THE *COMPLETE* BEGINNER'S GUIDE TO

WATER SKIING

by *Al Tyll*

Foreword by James G. Sylvester

Doubleday & Company, Inc., Garden City, New York

ISBN: 0-385-03572-1   TRADE
0-385-11349-8   PREBOUND

Library of Congress Catalog Card Number 69-15164

I dedicate this book to my good friend Ed Berner, who loves water skiing with a passion, and is himself a great credit to the sport.

ACKNOWLEDGMENTS

I have never met a nicer bunch of young people than the ones I photographed for this book. I thank them most of all for skiing so well for the pictures that I hope will help make this book easy to understand. I also thank them for being so generous with their time, and humor, and for never complaining when the water was cold or rough, or when I wanted a trick done "one more time." To Wayne Grimditch, Janie and Beth Peckinpaugh, Scott Loomis, Peter Knapp, Rit Forcier, and Paula Geitz, many, many thanks.

I am indebted to my wonderful wife Chris, and my dad and mother, Mr. and Mrs. Alfred E. Tyll, for their special assistance in boat driving, rigging the camera boat and tower, coordinating and organizing—and baby sitting for little Tracey while we were busy on the lake.

My deepest appreciation goes to Mike Amico of Cinema Beaulieu Camera Company for supplying the fine equipment and technical advice—not to mention donating two weeks of his vacation for the shooting and processing.

To Tom Hardman, editor of *The Water Skier* magazine, I am indebted for providing essential photographs and endless information regarding the American Water Ski Association, competition, record holders, and many other fine points. Those *Water Skier* magazines were my most valuable reference material.

To 1964 mixed doubles champions Bill and Marilyn Peirce, much appreciation for the chapter on mixed doubles. Your ideas and techniques are superb.

For their cooperation in supplying great towboats and photos for my use, my heartiest thanks to Ab Crosby of Hydrodyne Boats; George Dick of Correct Craft Boats; John Tuzee of Johnson Motors; and Tom Dorwin of Evinrude. And thanks to J. LeClair of Airguide Instrument Company, for the speedometers and photographs.

I am grateful to Bob Velzy and Frank Brownson of Taperflex Skis; to Bill Rutland of Cypress Gardens Skis; to Tony Kluge of Holdex Binders; and to Herb O'Brien of O'Brien Skis for their assistance in furnishing equipment and photographs.

Sincere appreciation goes to Jim Weyer of Weyer's Aqua Products, Inc., for his technical advice, photos, and other aid in compiling the chapter on kite flying; and to Pioneer Parachute Company for the information on Para-Sailing.

Heartfelt thanks to Jim Sylvester, able President of the American Water Ski Association, whose encouragement and assistance were so greatly appreciated by Chris and myself.

For their kind assistance, thanks to my fellow members of the Bantam Lake Ski Club, namely: Jim Parsons, George Sigiel (who loaned us his special concave saucer), Gary Lichtenstein, Harvey Dinerstein, Timmy Pusch, Warren Robbins, Glen Robbins, Mike Laurentano, and President Ed Boucher.

Thanks to my skiing pals and training buddies, Norm Boulris, Ben and Mary Walsh, Jason Brow, June and Howie Mitchell; Rose and "Bubby" Birk, and my able secretary, Muriel Rutkowski.

And very importantly, thanks to Stew Leonard for helping me become a champion in the first place!

FOREWORD

About ten years ago I watched a pleasant but serious young man leave the starting dock at the Eastern United States Water Ski Championships for his warmup run just before entering the trick course to compete in the men's trick event. The "warmup" consists of a three-minute period during which the skier adjusts boat speed and runs through several of his more difficult tricks to loosen his muscles and otherwise relax himself prior to entering the trick course for the real thing.

A crowd of several thousand watched in awe as the young skier flawlessly performed the most complicated and difficult trick skiing sequence they had ever seen. It was a dazzling spectacle of turns and spins by a highly tuned and exceptional athlete. After this amazing warmup routine, the skier entered the trick course for his first official pass. He fell on his second trick, completely ruining any chance to place in the event.

We in the crowd could only feel a complete sympathy at such a tragedy. The fallen skier, however, emerged from the water with a grin. He continued his one remaining trick run pass with perfect execution and grace, and skied back to the dock with an ear-to-ear smile for the crowd. It was an impressive display of good sportsmanship and competitive courage.

Such was my introduction to Al Tyll.

In succeeding years Al became the greatest trick skier and superstar the sport has ever known. He is an outstanding athlete. His record speaks for itself and does not need embellishment here. But there are qualities in Al Tyll that I do want to make known.

He has always been an inspiration to other, particularly younger, skiers. His sense of dedication, which is reinforced by his ready smile (have you noticed how few pictures there are of Al not smiling?) and winning ways with young people, have given encouragement to countless aspiring skiers. He has written excellent articles directed at young people about the sport of water skiing for such publications as *Boys' Life, The Water Skier,* and many others. He has trained some of our nation's top champions, and is recognized as one of the most capable ski trainers in the world.

In spite of his busy schedule, Al Tyll has always found the time to contribute his talent and sound judgment to the organized body of the sport—the American Water Ski Association. He has served with distinction on national committees and has been elected to regional office by the skier membership.

I am sure you will find this book interesting because it is written in the easy style that characterizes Al Tyll. He knows the sport well, and writes about it so naturally that it is as if he were talking with you on the dock next to his home in Bantam, Connecticut. This book is made even more valuable by the breathtaking quality of the photography, most of which was supervised by Al Tyll personally.

Chris Tyll, Al's lovely wife, and a proficient skier in her own right, also contributed much to this book. Her encouragement, which ranges from expert boat driving to being Al's best rooter at the national tournaments, was, I know, a major factor in the writing of the book.

It is with the greatest of pleasure that I recommend this book to both young and old. For the young, it represents a key to unlock summers of fun, combining physical fitness with recreation under sun and sky. For the old, it makes you younger—and you just never get too old to enjoy skiing. You see, that is the magic of water skiing.

James G. Sylvester
President, American Water Ski Association 1968–69
Hanover, Massachusetts
September 1968

CONTENTS

THE *COMPLETE* BEGINNER'S GUIDE TO
WATER SKIING

1. A date on skis. (Courtesy Correct Craft, Inc.)

CHAPTER ONE

The Fun of Water Skiing

There is hardly a sport that is fundamentally easier to learn than water skiing. With proper instruction, children two years old have learned to water ski; so have people in their seventies! You can experience the pleasures of the sport almost immediately, simply by following a few basic rules.

An estimated ten million Americans water ski each year. It's an excellent way to use the family boat—a pleasant and exciting addition to boating. And aside from pure gymnastics, no other sport is such a natural for body building and muscle toning. Take a close look at avid water skiers. You can bet they're in good shape.

What about falling? If you don't take a spill once in a while you're not learning much. After all, how can you improve without trying new tricks? Taking a dunking is just part of the sport. When a skier falls at the recommended beginner's speed of twenty-two to twenty-five miles per hour, the impact or jolt is hardly equal to a fall off a one-meter diving board. Should you go slalom skiing (at twenty-six to thirty-six miles per hour) or jumping (at twenty-six to thirty-five miles per hour), the water does get "harder," but you'll have gained experience by then and will know how to take falls more easily. In more than twenty-five years of sanctioning water skiing competition, the American Water Ski Association has not recorded a single fatality at a tournament.

Technically, water skiing can be practiced anywhere there is calm, open water. Fresh water is preferable to salt water because salt water tends to feel more slippery, or greasy, and its corrosive qualities are tougher on skis, binders, boats, and motors.

Rivers, lakes, and ponds—the calmer the better—are where most skiers congregate. Since a majority of the eight million recreational boats in the United States are used on weekends, weekdays are the best time to expect optimum water skiing conditions. To find the calmest water and to avoid crowds, go skiing in the morning before noon, or in the evening after 6:00 P.M., when afternoon breezes have diminished.

Diehard water skiers (the first to ski in the spring and the last to quit in the fall) who brave cold water, wear rubber suits to keep warm. These are the same as the suits worn by skin divers; however, skiers usually desire a looser fit, especially at the shoulder, elbow, and knee joints so that the suit can't hinder body motion. Neoprene "wet suits" of three-sixteenths inch thickness are best, and they can be purchased in most sporting goods stores.

The social aspects of the sport are unlimited, with over five hundred ski clubs in the United States. In Connecticut alone there are fifteen; New York state has seven; Massachusetts, eight; and Florida, fifteen.

If you are already a good water skier, you owe it to yourself to master at least one of the sport's exciting events. Maybe you're gymnastic and will want to try trick skiing. Do you like speed? Take up slalom. Are you rugged and looking for a real thrill? Try jumping.

Everyone should pursue at least one "action" sport during his lifetime. And water skiing is pure action.

CHAPTER TWO

History

About as many people have claimed to be the inventor of water skiing as have claimed to be the inventor of the automobile. Each lake or prominent water ski area seems to have its own "father of water skiing," and one often hears statements such as, "Why, back in 1930 we made our own water skis out of pine boards with old shoes nailed to 'em." So what else is new? Chronologically, here are some facts—and rumors!

It is rumored that in France, or Austria, or Switzerland back in the early 1900s a group of Alpine snow skiers doing some late spring skiing were schussing down a steep slope into a narrow gorge. A steep bank rose into a gentle drumlin on the other side, so the skiers would speed across the gorge, and up the other side.

But this afternoon the snow on the bottom of the gorge had melted into a narrow spit of water. Several skiers saw the water and either fell or stopped before dunking. One of them, however, saw the water too late and just froze into his schussing crouch, expecting the worst. To everyone's amazement, including the skier's, he didn't go in for a frigid swim. Instead his great speed carried him right across the surface to the other side. That's how some people say water skiing began. Well, it's possible. (The author saw it done at Killington Ski Area several years ago—considerably after water skiing was invented.)

It makes sense, though, that until boats capable of at least twenty miles per hour were developed, water skiing wasn't too common. Water skiing probably began as "aquaplaning" in the 1920s. One straight board about two feet by six was tied to the towboat by a rope. The rider stood on the aft end of the board holding onto a rope bridle attached to the front of the board. He got a thrilling, more or less uncontrollable ride behind the boat at eight to twelve miles per hour.

Later on, a sportsman named Fred Waller of Huntington, Long Island, split the board in two and placed one foot on each board. Then he experimented with longer (up to eight feet long) and narrower (four-inch to eight-inch) boards with separate bridle arrangements. But the boards were still tied to the boat.

The trick, of course, was to keep his feet on the boards, since binders had not yet been discovered. The rider would manipulate the bridles like reins, and by shifting his weight from side to side he managed to "steer" the boards to some extent. In 1924, Waller applied for a patent for what he called "Dolphin Akwa-Skees." He was the first to refer to this amazing new sport as skiing on water.

Almost simultaneously, Waller began working on a pair of "Skees" containing binders for the feet. Instead of the skis being attached to the boat by means of a rope and bridle, the rider held a wooden handle tied to the end of the line. However, Waller claimed that these were much harder to ride and control than his unconventional Akwa-Skees, which had no binders.

Rumor also has it that back around 1929 a Count Maximilian Pulaski, who was something of a ladies' man about the French Riviera, frequently took his girl friends on aquaplaning dates. He and some cohorts built a pair of narrow aquaplanes bearing rubber foot binders, and soon that became the vogue sport at the elegant playground.

There are also stories of the officers of the Chasseurs Alpins of the 11th Regiment of Annecy in the French Alps, who indulged in skijoring, being pulled on snow skis behind a horse. These rugged fellows didn't want to stop skijoring when summer came, but tried it on water while being towed by a horse running along the beach. After continual dunkings, they mounted their boots via leather thongs on wider curved boards than their regular snow skis. They eventually succeeded in water skiing, and later supposedly used boats as the towing vehicle. However, another water skiing pioneer in Europe, André Coutau of Geneva, Switzerland, doubts this claim because in 1929 there were no fast speedboats in that area of France or Switzerland. Coutau claims that he rode the first true water skis in southern France in 1929 or 1930, and that they were nine feet long.

Then in 1966, all these claims took a dunking. Margaret Crimmins, a writer for the St. Paul *Pioneer Press,* while on vacation in Lake City, Minnesota, spied a strange-looking pair of skis in a bathhouse and asked the bathhouse manager if she could try them out. He agreed, in exchange for a little publicity in her newspaper, claiming that they were the world's first water skis.

"As for the skis," said Mrs. Crimmins, "it was a wild experience on them. I plopped twice but got up on the third try behind a forty-horsepower rig. The skis were really difficult to hold together because of their length. Two teen-age boys went out with me. One got up and skied for a short distance (about a hundred yards, just as I had done) but the other never did make it."

Mrs. Crimmins wrote a column on her experience which led to the uncovering of a brand new set of facts:

It seems that in 1922, two years before Fred Waller ever tried skiing, Ralph W. Samuelson, then an adventurous eighteen-year-old daredevil, skied on prototype conventional water skis before many witnesses at Lake City, Minnesota, and subsequently put on free one-man skiing exhibitions every summer, for fifteen years! His first skis were eight feet long and nine inches wide, weighing fifteen pounds. He warped their leading tips by steaming them. His binders were merely two-inch straps, with no heelpieces. He continually looked for faster towboats and soon skied at thirty-five miles per hour. But he wanted still more speed. Finally, he convinced a Northwest Airlines pilot, Walter Bullock, to tow him behind a World War I surplus Curtis MF Flying Boat—at speeds up to eighty miles per hour. Samuelson states: "Bullock and I got together as two nuts, I guess. He'd take passengers for a ride and then pull me for a show."

Even this wasn't daring enough! In 1925, Samuelson constructed a slanted "float" five feet high, greased the ramp surface, and became the first man to make water ski jumps. His amazing jumps were fifty to sixty feet long!

In the late 1920s Samuelson put on one-man ski shows throughout Minnesota and Michigan, and each fall in Palm Beach, Florida. He recalls, "A lot of wealthy people from the French Riviera used to watch my exhibitions at Palm Beach. Some of them were

2. The father of water skiing, Ralph Samuelson, shows his original water skis to Ben Simons, who witnessed Samuelson's skiing in 1922. (Courtesy American Water Ski Association)

3. Samuelson skied behind this Curtis Flying Boat in 1925, at speeds near eighty miles per hour. (Courtesy American Water Ski Association)

4. Samuelson giving a one-man ski show in 1925. (Courtesy American Water Ski Association)

particularly fascinated with skiing on water, and they undoubtedly took the idea back to Europe with them." (This could explain how Count Pulaski got hold of the idea.)

To permanently seal the fact that Ralph Samuelson is the real father of water skiing, on December 9, 1965, the Chamber of Commerce of Lake City, Minnesota, sent a letter to the American Water Ski Association, signed by eight witnesses who saw Samuelson water skiing on Lake Pepin in 1922. As for Samuelson, he's stayed quietly in the background for all these years running a turkey farm. Semiretired now, at sixty-five, he works summers as a Minnesota highway department maintenance engineer.

CHAPTER THREE

The Towboat

Any boat that can pull a skier out and over the water can theoretically be used for water skiing. But not all boats are good ski towboats. Usually boats between fourteen and twenty feet long with plenty of "pull power," speed, roominess, and maneuverability are suitable for water skiing.

"Pull power" is a snappy-strong acceleration capable of pulling a skier out of the water on a deep water start without bogging or straining.

The amount of speed required depends on the kind of skiing you intend to do. A boat that can tow at twenty-two miles per hour is sufficient to give the casual skier a nice ride. However, should that skier decide to kick off one ski, he may bog the boat down to twenty or even nineteen, and that wouldn't be too comfortable. Most skiers today buy boats capable of towing a skier at thirty to forty miles per hour.

Roominess is desirable since there must be sufficient space for one or more observers, extra ropes, skis, life preservers, boarding ladders, towels, and other paraphernalia.

Good boat maneuverability helps you return to a fallen skier promptly. After all, the water may be cold or the skier might be winded. He wants to ski, not swim. Besides, the longer you leave him in the water the more you increase his chances of getting hit by another boat, especially on busy days.

There are now three kinds of boats popularly used for skiing: outboards, inboards, and inboard-outboards.

5. Outboard ski towboat: A small boat with a wide transom and good-sized outboard motor.

OUTBOARDS:

An outboard boat has a motor bolted to the transom, with the lower unit which drives the propeller sticking into the water. The motor is actually outside, or "outboard" the boat's hull. Outboard motors range from 2½ to 125 horsepower. One can easily water ski behind a thirty-five-hp motor on, say, a fourteen-foot hull. Of course, pull power would be minimal, but standard skiing or trick skiing could be enjoyed.

In tournaments, two powerful outboard motors (usually 100 hp each) are mounted on an eighteen-foot hull, having a transom wide enough to accommodate them. Because horsepower is doubled, and two propellers are turning in the water, these "twin rigs" have plenty of pull power. Even the strongest slalom skiers cannot slow them down much.

Most outboard motors are two-cycle engines using gasoline mixed with oil. They are not as economical to run as many people

think. Some 75- to 125-horsepower outboard motors used for skiing guzzle six to nine gallons per hour; and remember, one quart
of oil has to be mixed with every twelve gallons of gasoline burned.
At tournaments, some outboard twin rigs have burned one hundred
gallons of gasoline a day! They're superb towboats—if you can afford to run them!

Fourteen- to sixteen-footers with fifty-horsepower outboard motors make snappy little towboats capable of over thirty miles per
hour, although slalom skiers will slow them down when they cut.
Outboards of seventy-five or one hundred horsepower will drink
lots of gas and oil, but allow you to attain skiing speeds of thirty-
five miles per hour or more and to do most kinds of water skiing
behind them, including barefoot skiing.

Outboards require more maintenance than inboards, but because
they weigh less they are generally easier to trailer around and
put in and out of the water. Their lower units can be tilted up out
of the water permitting safe, damage-free launching and trailering.

INBOARDS:

An inboard boat contains its engine permanently inside the hull.
Almost all inboard engines are the four-cycle, reciprocating type,
burning straight gasoline. You do not mix oil with the gas, but
must check the oil crankcase level periodically, just as you do with
a car.

Most inboards are now sold with engines of one hundred horsepower in them so that almost any inboard can easily tow a skier
for ordinary skiing. The engine is usually mounted in the center of
the boat behind the front seat. It is covered with a "motor box"
or "engine cover," or "middeck" which can be used as a seat by
passengers. In the utility type of inboard, there is room all around
the engine for passengers, skis, ropes, and other skiing equipment.

Four-cycle marine engines seem to be much more efficient than
two-cycle outboard motors. A 135-horsepower V-8 inboard engine
has been known to burn only as much gasoline per hour as a
thirty-five-horsepower outboard motor—both being used for skiing

6. Inboard ski towboat designed by the author: Note the ski tow pylon in the center of the boat. Lots of room inboard. Observer's seat faces aft. This boat has 210 horsepower and consumes only three to four gallons of gasoline per hour. (Courtesy Correct Craft, Inc.)

—and hardly any oil. That means four times as much power on the same quantity of fuel! Averaging out, though, you can figure a ratio of three to one (for example, a seventy-five-horsepower outboard will burn approximately as much gas and oil as a 210-horsepower inboard V-8). For this reason many tournament directors and sponsoring clubs prefer inboard towboats. The tremendous saving on gas and oil can make the difference between breaking even, or going into the red.

Because they are generally heavier boats, inboards tend to give a smoother, steadier pull, and leave behind higher, more definite wakes than outboards. Some skiers like low wakes because they seem easier to cross; others like to jump off higher wakes. In tournaments, jumpers and slalom competitors prefer as little wake as possible, while trick skiers like medium-sized, sharply defined wakes for their wake tricks. I have heard many discussions, pro and con, regarding the wake situation, and have come to one conclusion: It all depends on what you're used to. Besides, at slalom and jumping speeds most wakes flatten out anyway.

Modern wide-beamed sixteen- to eighteen-foot inboards of 135 horsepower or more make economical, trouble-free ski towboats, and have good water skiing wakes.

Generally, inboards are harder to dock or maneuver at slow speeds than outboards. The driver can only change direction by means of his rudder, as the prop and shaft stay rigidly fixed under the keel. (When maneuvering an outboard, the whole engine turns, including the direction of the prop.) However, at speeds above ten miles per hour many inboards maneuver better than outboards —and with little or no cavitation.*

Inboards trailer all right, but launching is finicky since the shaft, prop, rudder, and strut cannot be tipped up out of harm's way. A good, rockfree launching ramp is recommended.

INBOARD-OUTBOARDS:

A few years ago, inboard-outboards hit the scene, utilizing both principles—the economy and power of a four-cycle engine driving an outboard unit that can easily be tipped up for trailering, inspection, safe launching, or beaching.

Per horsepower unit, inboard-outboards have greater speed than inboards, yet are able to equal their torque or pull power. They are being used by more and more skiers; in fact, one manufacturer is now making a special inboard-outboard tournament ski boat especially designed for official tournament use. Inboard-outboard units are powered by as high as three-hundred-horsepower engines.

BOAT EQUIPMENT:

A good towboat should contain a ski tow hitch, or pylon, to which the tow rope is connected. In outboards, the hitch should be securely installed two to five feet in front of the transom (or

---

* Cavitation can occur when a boat turns sharply, thereby tipping up on its side and allowing the propeller to come out of the water.

7. Inboard-outboard tournament ski towboat: A low, fast, powerful, wide-transomed boat with 200 horsepower. The lower unit can be tilted up for shallow water, trailering, etc. This boat burns only about 3½ gallons of gasoline per hour, holds speed very accurately, and has plenty of room inside. (Courtesy Hydrodyne Boats)

engine). In inboards, a towing pylon is usually installed just in front of the engine. Theoretically it should be close to the center-turning axis of the boat, so no matter how hard a skier pulls or cuts, it will not rock or veer the boat off course.

A word of caution here—especially to owners of lightweight twelve- to fourteen-foot boats with small outboard engines who use plain towing bridles attached to the transom. Never tie the ski rope to one side of the transom; should the skier decide to cut way out to one side while the boat is turning toward that side, his pulling could capsize it. Instead, use a towing bridle attached to cleats placed on top of the transom on either side of the outboard motor, allowing just enough room for it to turn inside the "V" of the bridle. Better yet, invest in a good ski tow hitch.

DESIRED INSTRUMENTATION:

The most important function of the ski towboat is good control. The steering wheel should move freely and positively, without

play. Keep your steering mechanism checked for worn spots, rubbing, and malfunctions. A runaway, unsteerable boat is a night-
mare.

Second, the throttle. It should be positive, with little or no
"slop" or play. The slightest movement of the throttle should result
in either deceleration or acceleration. Good throttle-to-carburetor
linkage is a must, especially for tournament drivers whose speeds
are constantly being checked against stopwatches. To trick skiers
accurate speeds are essential. Variances of as little as one-half mile
per hour could cause them to fall during a delicate trick. (And if
they suspect it, you'll hear about it.)

8. This speedometer has a large,
easily readable face with wide
spaces between indicator lines, enabling the driver to set speeds
within one-half mile per hour.
(Courtesy Airguide Instrument Co.)

That's where a good marine speedometer comes in handy. Most
manufacturers say they calibrate their instruments before shipping
them out. Even so, before you place any credence in the accuracy
of your newly installed speedometer, time the boat through a
slalom course with a stopwatch. (See table on page 70.) Good
speedometers have an adjustment screw for recalibration. Some
may be accurate plus or minus one mile per hour in the fifteen to twenty-five miles per hour range, but be off by three miles
per hour at thirty-five! The bigger the face of the speedometer (with
larger denomination spaces) the easier it will be to maintain an accurate reading.

9. Dashboard on a ski towboat. Note the two speedometers mounted in look-through steering wheel. Also note convex rear-view mirror.

THE RPM FALLACY:

Many boats have tachometers showing engine revolutions per minute. Sometimes, drivers use rpm readings as indications of speed. They'll say, "I was taking you at 3200." Well, what does that mean? Thirty-two hundred in relation to what? One boat at 3200 engine rpm may be doing twenty-eight miles per hour, while another boat revving at 3200 rpm could be traveling thirty-five miles per hour. Besides, a boat with just a driver in it at 3200 rpm may be doing thirty-five miles per hour, while that same boat loaded with two observers and towing a skier might only go thirty-two miles per hour! Watch out for the rpm fallacy.

SAFETY EQUIPMENT:

Naturally, obey your state and Coast Guard regulations. Have a fire extinguisher, life preserves, and a boarding ladder in the boat at all times. A large curved-convex type of rear-view mirror is very handy to give the driver an idea of what the skier is doing, and prevents the driver from taking his eyes "off the road."

SIGNALS TO BOAT DRIVER

A

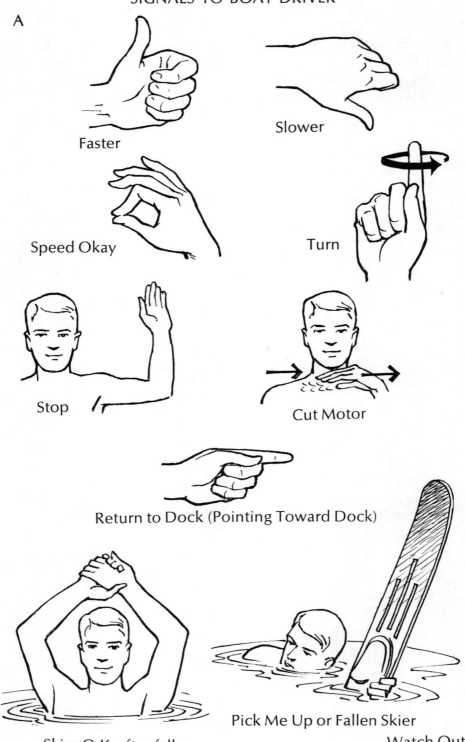

Faster

Slower

Speed Okay

Turn

Stop

Cut Motor

Return to Dock (Pointing Toward Dock)

Skier O.K. after fall

Pick Me Up or Fallen Skier
—Watch Out

CHAPTER FOUR

An Important Lesson in Towboat Driving

This is the most important chapter in this book, and it could insure a long, happy future for you and your water skiing friends. Water skiing itself is extremely safe; but the driving—there's the rub! Most "water skiing" accidents are caused by the negligence of the boat driver. So study the following carefully:

First, familiarize yourself with the waters on which you are boating. Are there underwater obstacles? Shallow areas? Strong currents? If so, stay away from them. Except when starting or landing a skier, stay in water over five feet deep.

Second, make sure your boat is mechanically safe.

Third, don't tow a skier behind an unfamiliar boat unless you've learned its sensitivities and performance characteristics. Conversely, don't ski behind a strange driver without first knowing or checking out his driving ability and experience. I always go out in the boat with a new driver to show him how the boat should be driven.

Fourth, agree on a communication system (see Diagram A). Discuss desired speeds, length of ski ride wanted, and the skiing area preferred.

Since an observer should always be in the boat, include him in all these conversations and/or instructions. And, if you're the observer, don't sightsee. It's your job to watch the skier at all times.

When starting a skier from deep water, a driver should make sure the skier is in proper position and ready before he accelerates the boat. When set, the skier should yell "Hit it!" The driver should accelerate gradually until just before the desired speed is reached, then back off and adjust to that speed. In a comfortable deep-water start, the skis surface in two to three seconds.

When starting a skier from a dock, the driver should idle the boat forward as he is pulling away from the dock. About one second before the rope tightens, he should begin gradual accelera-tion.

RECOMMENDED SPEEDS FOR TOWING BEGINNERS

Skier's Weight	Recommended Boat Speed
30–50 lbs.	10–15 mph
50–80 lbs.	13–20 mph
80–120 lbs.	18–22 mph
120 and over lbs.	22–24 mph

(Later, as the novice becomes more proficient, he will select his own speed.)

Use common sense when towing a skier. Let's say your boat is fifteen feet long, and you are using a seventy-five-foot towrope. You are driving a vehicle ninety feet long! But how wide is your "vehicle"? Well, the skier can reach seventy-five feet to the left and seventy-five feet to the right, so theoretically your vehicle is ninety feet long by 150 feet wide. Should a boat be driven closer to any object than seventy-five feet, the skier might be endangered, for he is relying on the driver to keep him out of trouble. Suppose for some reason the skier lets go after cutting to one side. His mo-mentum could carry him another seventy-five or more feet beyond that point. So, why risk the skier's life, limb, and pursuit of happy water skiing! *When towing a skier try not to drive your boat closer than 150 feet from any other object, vessel, marker, or shoreline.* (Of course, this may not be possible when water skiing in a narrow strip of water, such as a river; in that case, stay in the middle, away from shore.)

BRINGING THE ROPE BACK TO A FALLEN SKIER:

When maneuvering around a fallen skier (then a swimmer), *idle* up to him and always pass him on your side (the driver's side) of the boat, to keep him under constant observation. In other words, a

B

BRINGING THE ROPE BACK TO A FALLEN SKIER

This diagram assumes that the boat being used
is a right hand drive—that is, as in most boats,
the driver is seated on the right (starboard) side.

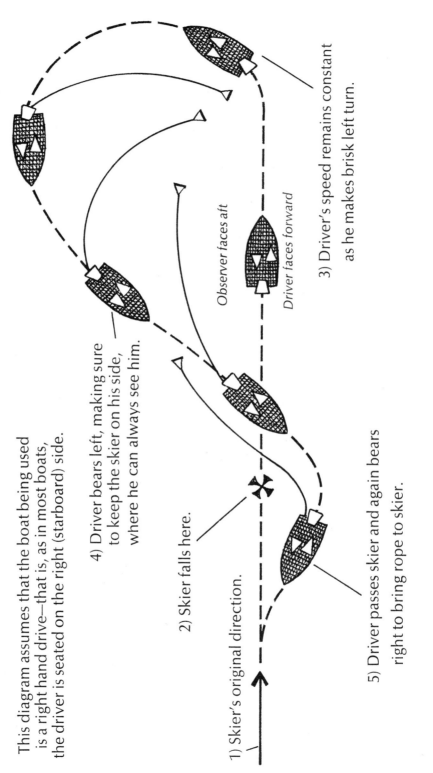

3) Driver's speed remains constant
as he makes brisk left turn.

Observer faces aft

Driver faces forward

4) Driver bears left, making sure
to keep the skier on his side,
where he can always see him.

2) Skier falls here.

1) Skier's original direction.

5) Driver passes skier and again bears
right to bring rope to skier.

driver sitting on the starboard (right) side should pass to the left of the fallen skier. There is also a trick to bringing the rope right back to him—so he doesn't have to swim for it.

In Diagram B, the driver is seated on the starboard side of the boat. The skier falls at X. The driver briskly turns the boat left in a 180-degree half circle and returns, making sure to keep the skier on his right. As he idles past the skier he turns slightly to the right. Since the free floating handle-end of the rope has a tendency to drift toward the center of any circle or curve the boat makes, it is thus brought directly to the skier.

Always keep a boarding ladder in the boat. When skiers fall and decide to call it quits, they're usually exhausted. Some don't have the energy to pull themselves in over the gunwale without a ladder, especially once-a-year skiers. The motor should always be shut off when a skier is climbing aboard.

MAKING A TURN:

A skier gets the best ride when the boat is traveling in a straight line, since he has no centrifugal forces or side pulls to compensate for. And, don't forget, a boat makes waves. After three or four circles, around even a "mill pond," its calm water could become a writhing mess. So use the barbell course (see Diagram C).

When the boat must turn, the driver should signal the skier to prepare for it. The driver first turns a bit to the left, before making a neat right-hand-turn circle sixty to eighty yards in diameter, ending it approximately where it started—in the center of his previous track or wake. He then heads along this line in the opposite direc-

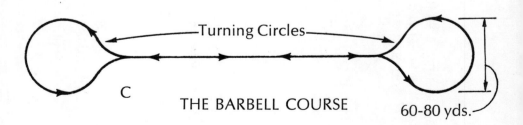

C   THE BARBELL COURSE   60-80 yds.

tion, missing all the rough water caused by his previous pass. On reaching the other end, he repeats the process, coming back in the same course. The longer your straight path, the better, but of course that depends on the size of your practice area or lake. In tournaments, official drivers always follow this pattern to give competitors "the best water possible."

LANDING A SKIER:

Many drivers seem to think that when a skier wants to be brought back to shore they have to drive him within six inches of the float or dock or beach he came from. This puts the skier in danger—especially an inexperienced one. Never drive the boat closer than 150 feet from shore when letting off a skier. Chances are that when the skier lets go, his momentum will carry him in toward shore anyway. Better to have him wind up swimming or wading a few feet, than tumbling up a beach or crashing into a dock. (This is how many so-called "water skiing" injuries have occurred.) Also, maintain a constant speed when letting off a skier. If you decrease speed just as the skier is letting go, or preparing to let go, you may throw him off balance. When the skier is off, stop the boat and pull in the rope. And remember, it is not a good idea to drive the boat for even short distances with the towrope dragging in the water. First of all it's rough on the rope and handle, and secondly you might just hook onto a dock, piling, raft, or swimmer and cause serious damage or injury.

CHAPTER FIVE

Basic Standard Skiing

THE ROPE AND HANDLE:

The rope length used for standard water skiing is seventy-five feet. One-quarter-inch diamond braid polyethylene or polypropylene having a breaking strength of more than eight hundred pounds are recommended because they are lightweight and rotproof and they float.

Polyethylene will stretch at first but soon "sets" and becomes quite stable.

However, polypropylene (the official material sanctioned by the American Water Ski Association) has a more elastic quality. For instance, a strong skier can stretch a seventy-five-foot polypropylene line two feet during a cut, but it will recoil back to its original length.

In 1964, when the AWSA first started using polypropylene, some slalom competitors unaccustomed to the new material were yanked right out of their skis while executing strong cuts at high speeds. They were politely told to start practicing with the new line, and after a little experience with it many skiers actually felt the line was advantageous.

In that same year three young women, Barbara Klack, Dicksie Ann Hoyt, and Liz Allan broke the one-hundred-foot mark in the women's and girl's jumping events. Before using the polypropylene line none of the girls had jumped that far, so most observers felt that the recoil of the rope gave them the extra footage.

However, in trick skiing, with its quick tugs and difficult rope handling, a non-recoil line such as braided polyethylene is preferable. And, to insure absolutely no "give," many competitors use ropes of five-sixteenths inch and even three-eighths inch thickness.

Years ago many water skiers used double handles, but now the single handle has been widely adopted. Handles are usually constructed of hardwood, aluminum, plastic, rubber, or combinations thereof. Handle diameters vary from one inch (for small hands) to one and a quarter inches (for larger hands); lengths, from eleven to eighteen inches.

The best handles consist of an aluminum core, coated with soft cellular neoprene; they are both strong and comfortable.

For ordinary water skiing, use the "knuckles-up" grip (see Picture 10). This natural grip is comfortable for relaxed water skiing. During strenuous cuts or pulls such as in slalom and jumping, use the "baseball-bat" grip. In this grip each hand grasps the handle from the opposite direction, providing a firmer hold.

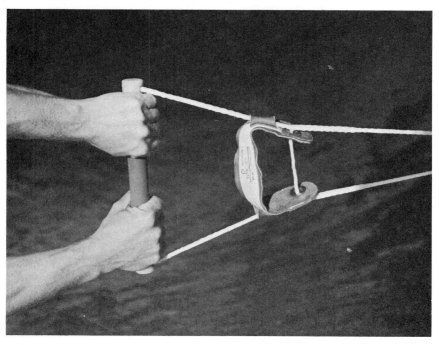

10. "Knuckles-up" grip.

11. "Baseball-bat" grip—the strongest grip.

STANDARD SKIS:

Most standard water skis are five or six feet long, six to seven inches wide, and one-half to three-quarters inch thick. Each ski has a curved leading tip, a foot binder approximately in the middle of the ski, and a small stabilizing keel at the tail to keep the ski tracking well.

Skis are manufactured out of wood, fiberglass, or melamine, or combinations thereof. Naturally, they must be durable and they must float. Standard skis vary in shape between the square back with straight parallel sides and the banana design, which has curved sides and tapers almost to a point at the tail.

"Square backs" can carry more weight at slower speeds and track well. They are recommended for beginners. The more stream-

12. Standard water skis. Back binder mounted on one ski makes it a fine slalom ski. Combination pairs like this save you money, as you are actually getting a slalom ski and a pair, in one. (Courtesy Superior Sports Specialties)

lined "bananas" handle better at higher speeds, are easier to accelerate and decelerate, and are more maneuverable.

RECOMMENDED LENGTHS FOR STANDARD SKIS

Skier's Weight	Ski Length	Ski Width
30–80 lbs.	52″	5″–6″
70–200 lbs.	66″	6½″
170 and over lbs.	68″–72″	6½″–8″

LIFE VESTS AND SKI BELTS:

You should be a competent swimmer if you are to water ski. Nevertheless, novice water skiers should always wear some type of flotation, such as the popular ski vests and ski belts.

Ski belts are usually six to eight inches wide and a couple of inches thick. They're fine for water skiing providing you're careful when you buckle them. Remember, a ski belt is no use to you if it comes off after a hard spill.

The ski vest is a must for all high-speed skiing such as slalom, jumping, barefoot, racing, or kite flying. It affords more protection for the skier's upper torso during hard spills and floats him higher in the water because it contains more flotation material. The best ski vests and ski belts are made of polyvinylchloride, a soft, comfortable substance which is very tear-resistant and durable.

THE AL TYLL SUCCESS FACTOR:

Before each new set of instructions, I will indicate how many attempts or tries it should take the average person to learn the

13. Here Scotty Loomis wears a ski belt, while Pete Knapp wears a ski vest, which are mandatory flotation for slalom, jumping, barefoot, and fast skiing of all kinds.

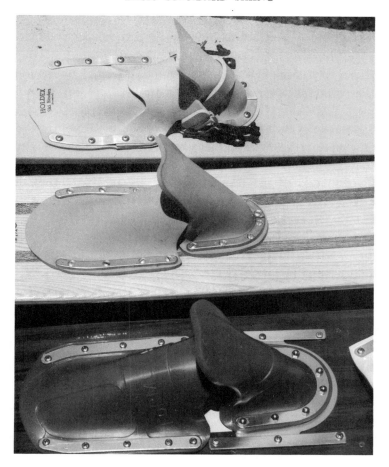

14. Water ski binders.

> *Top:* This binder of pure gum rubber with adjustable
> hold-down straps and reinforcing piece across the
> heel fits almost like a shoe. (Courtesy Tony Kluge,
> Holdex Binders)

> *Center:* Fixed tournament binder: you buy the ski with
> only the front toepiece mounted. Then you mount
> the heelpiece on the ski according to your foot size.
> (Courtesy Cypress Gardens Skis)

> *Bottom:* This is actually a fixed binder, but you can ad-
> just it simply by removing the center screws of the
> heel rails. It's good for kids with fast-growing feet.
> Binder material is Formulastic. (Courtesy Superior
> Sports Specialties)

type of skiing or trick discussed. This does not mean that after you first succeed you won't fall again on the same trick. (I guarantee you will!) It is just an estimate of how soon you can first expect to accomplish it. If you don't succeed within the success factor, reread the instructions. You must be doing something wrong!

I suggest that you learn each type of skiing or trick in the order recommended in this book. Otherwise the success factor may prove inaccurate. It has been carefully calculated, taking into consideration the difficulty of the tricks and the skill of the learner. Each set of instructions is designed to prepare you for the next trick.

SKI BINDERS—ADJUSTABLE VS. FIXED:

Your water ski binders connect you with your skis. The better the connection, the more control you'll have over the skis. The slightest amount of play or looseness, pinch or pain, can hamper your performance.

Water skis generally come with adjustable binders already attached. However, champion or connoisseur skiers like to buy "blanks" on which they mount their own custom, fixed binders, for their particular foot size. Naturally, the latter binders are best, because they are like your own shoes. (They also prevent a lot of moochers from using your favorite skis.)

Popular binder materials are pure gum rubber, Formulastic,

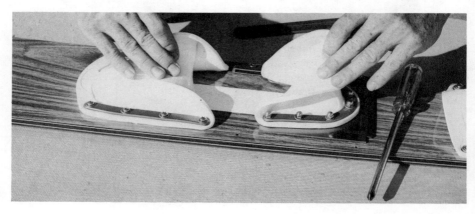

15. Placing non-skid tape inside the binders underfoot affords a firmer stance on the ski itself.

and neoprene. Adjustable binders are designed to accommodate the range of average foot sizes, but before you buy water skis, slip your feet into the binders to see if they pinch or hurt. Always wet either your feet or the skis before slipping into binders; otherwise they'll seem loose when wet. Try to avoid adjustable binders with cheap, flimsy adjustment mechanisms. And watch out for binder hardware with sharp edges or bolts or wing nuts sticking out; these can result in bad cuts. For better control of your skis, stick non-skid tape on the ski inside the binder. This should help to keep your foot from sliding around.

When adjusting your binders remember one thing: The tighter the better. Don't worry about them not coming off should you take a hard spill. They'll come off.

RECOMMENDED SIGNALS BETWEEN SKIER AND DRIVER:

Even before you put water skis on your feet for the first time, take a couple of minutes to get acquainted with the following hand signals—and make sure your driver understands them too! (See Diagram A.)

LET'S GO SKIING! GETTING UP ON TWO SKIS:

Success Factor: 1 to 6 tries

Use a good standard pair of water skis suitable for your weight (see table of recommended lengths on page 27). Before entering the water, adjust your binders for a snug fit. Put on a ski belt or ski vest, making sure it is properly buckled. Then wade out into waist-deep water and put on your skis.

Grasp the handle and lower yourself into the water, pulling your knees in toward your chest. Keep your arms straight and hold the rope between your two ski tips, which should be sticking out of the water, about a foot apart. Holding yourself rigid in this position, tell the driver to put the boat "in gear," beginning a slow, forward idle.

Remain frozen in the starting crouch as you feel yourself being pulled forward. If you have no problem holding position yell "Hit it," so the driver can begin acceleration.

At eight to ten miles per hour your skis will begin to surface. Stay rigid, keeping your arms straight. Many beginners have a tendency to pull in on the rope. Don't! Just try to keep your weight over your binders.

Should you topple to one side or another when starting, you're not in a good, stable, crouch. Stay lower. If you fall forward, with your skis spreading apart, you're not holding them rigidly parallel or compensating (leaning) against the boat's pull properly. Falling backward indicates too much lean against the pull of the boat; or maybe you've pulled in your arms attempting to stand up too soon. When you feel that a fall is inevitable, let go of the handle and just relax.

At twenty miles per hour, your skis will track high and easily. Don't try to stand up too soon. Stay in the low, vertical crouch for a few moments until you get your "ski legs" and a feeling of confidence.

When the boat speed levels off (and it should at around twenty-two miles per hour for your first ride), straighten up slowly, making sure your arms are straight and your skis parallel, about a foot apart. Gradually straighten your back until it's comfortable, but keep a slight bend in your knees. If you encounter other boat waves or rough water, bending your knees will help absorb the "bumps," and crouching low will lessen your chances of spilling. Ride directly behind the boat and don't try crossing the wakes

16, 17, 18, 19. Scotty demonstrates a deep-water start on two skis.

right away. You should not ski more than about five minutes the first time.

When you wish to stop skiing, either let go out in the water, or signal the driver "Back home." If he is a good driver, he won't bring you in too close to shore. Remember, at twenty miles per hour you could drift or "coast" another forty to sixty feet before sinking into the water, so let go of the rope a good distance from shore. "Swim or wade the rest of the way and live to ski another day."

HOW TO TURN OR "STEER" WATER SKIS:

Simply lean in the direction you wish to travel. For instance, leaning to the left puts more weight on the left edges of your skis, causing them to cut in that direction. To make a sharp turn, you must brace yourself against the pull of the boat and lean harder. When cutting hard or turning sharply on two skis, it is wise to stay low, in a crouch, because you'll gain speed rapidly.

STARTING FROM THE DOCK:

Success Factor: 1 to 4 tries

This is a very convenient way to start off. Many skiers feel it is simpler than starting from the water. It is physically easier but requires a certain knack, which comes with practice.

Simply sit on the edge of the dock with your skis dangling in the water, keeping their tips up, parallel and about a foot apart.

20, 21, 22. Two-ski dock start: Scotty keeps a slight bend in his arms to absorb the impact of the boat's sudden pull as the rope tightens.

Grasp the handle with both hands, arms slightly bent. Ready yourself for a slight jerk as the rope tightens, and let it pull you off the dock. Stay low in a vertical crouch, directly over your skis. When this start is performed correctly (by both driver and skier), you'll hardly wet your ankles.

A SKI TRAINER:

In 1962, a champion water skier, Stew Leonard of Norwalk, Connecticut, invented a simple but ingenious little device designed especially for those who have trouble staying in a low crouch starting position, or holding their skis rigidly. This ski trainer attaches to your ski rope. You merely slip it over your ski tips and clamp down. Automatically, your body, your skis, and the ski trainer become a solid, low, compact towing unit. Very rarely does it fail to get the beginner up on the first try!

DO'S AND DON'TS FOR BEGINNERS:

DO: Wear a ski belt or life vest.
      Watch where you are going at all times.
      Let go of the rope when falling.
      Ski with advanced skiers.
      Take certified instruction if you can get it.
      Use new modern equipment.
      After a fall, clasp both hands over your head, signaling
          you are okay.

DON'T: Ski too long the first few times, especially if you're an
             older person, or are out of shape.
         Ski too close to other boats, obstacles, or the shoreline.
         Ski directly ahead of another boat. (Suppose you fell?)
         Attempt fast landings directly toward docks or shore.
         Ski doubles with different length ropes.
         Put any part of your body through the rope bridle.

WATER SKIING AND YOUR PHYSICAL CONDITION:

Adults who have never water skied before will feel muscles they didn't know they had—the next day! That's why they shouldn't

23. The ski trainer slips over Tommy Leonard's ski tips . . .

24. . . . . making him squat nice and low as he pulls down on the handle, clamping the skis together.

25. On surfacing, he releases the down pressure on the handle, allowing the ski trainer to slide off his ski tips.

26. Tommy straightens up slowly, and the trainer becomes a regular towbar. (Courtesy Skee Trainer, Inc.)

ski longer than five minutes the first time out. After waiting an hour or so, they can go out again—but should call it quits for that day after the second time out. (Even I can "feel it" the first time out in the spring, after laying off for the winter. So can baseball and football players after their first day's training.)

Teen-agers and children are a different story. They can ski all day and never even breathe hard. So, judge yourselves accordingly and remember: Everyone has a limit.

Standard water skiing, slalom skiing, and jumping develop and harden muscles in your ankles, legs, back, arms, neck, wrists, and fingers. Trick skiing develops these muscles, plus every other muscle in your body, because it is so gymnastic and calisthenic. There isn't a body-building course available that trims unwanted weight, develops the body, and helps build stamina and endurance as easily as water skiing. And all the time you're having fun. What more can you ask?

CROSSING THE WAKE:

Success Factor: 1 to 2 tries

The boat wake is the watery track left by the boat. It is bounded on each side by a small wave caused by the boat parting the water's

27, 28, 29. Crossing the wake: Be sure to bend your knees.

surface. For the purposes of this book let's call these waves the "left wake" and "right wake," one on either side of the boat's path. Should you want to cross the left wake, lean in that direction and crouch low, as if you were bracing for some rough water. Don't stop on top of the wake, because you might get hung up on it—one ski on either side. Cross it with some momentum and continue skiing to a point twenty to thirty feet outside the wake, always maintaining a low center of gravity. Then ski back in again. After you've repeated that several times, try crossing the right wake. Next cross them both in one direction and then the other. Lo and behold, you're skiing a slalom pattern! Remember, practice makes perfect.

JUMPING THE WAKES:

Success Factor: "very easy"—1 try

Some skiers can get three or four feet in the air jumping the wakes. Of course, this depends on the wakes, the speed of the boat, and the skier's technique. With a good, fast cut, from out-

30, 31, 32. Jumping the wake: Scotty pops off the crest of the wake, but makes sure to land with his weight directly over his binders.

side in, you can easily clear both wakes. Since most boat wakes have a steeper angle on the outside, they form a better "jump" if approached from that direction.

To learn wake jumping, ski to the outside of the wake. Using the "baseball-bat" grip, pull in on the handle, crouch very low, and cut. When you hit the wake, straighten your knees, popping upward. When airborne, keep your ski tips up so they won't dig in and spill you forward on landing. Try to develop a certain style or form as experienced ski jumpers do. For instance, when airborne, you might adopt a straight soldier style, or be bent forward at the waist, jumper style. For a solid landing, bend at the knees and waist, keeping your skis a foot apart and parallel.

MULTIPLE OR GROUP SKIING:

There are several important points to remember when two or more skiers want to ski behind the same boat simultaneously.

First, adjust each rope length to make sure they are equal.

Second, agree on a procedure to follow should one skier fall. Either have a pickup boat following a good distance behind, ready to pick up fallen skiers; or, agree that if one skier falls, the towboat will immediately return and start him again from the water. (Of course, this necessitates dunking the remaining skiers, but that's the breaks.)

If you use the pickup boat system, the observer in the boat should quickly pull in the empty rope, hand over hand, letting the loose rope fall in the bottom of the boat as he retrieves it. Group skiing can result in pretty bad rope tangles, so try to keep the ropes separated.

When starting, each skier should hold his rope neatly coiled to prevent the separate ropes from entangling each other. As the boat idles out, taking up slack, the skiers should pay out the ropes carefully, keeping them apart.

While skiing, each skier must constantly watch the others, letting them know when and where he intends to swerve or turn. Rough body collisions are possible, should one skier be turning left while the other is turning right. Take three skiers, for example. The middle skier should stay inside the wakes, the left skier to the left of the wakes, and the right skier to the right of the wakes.

About this business of using different length ropes, so that you can jump each other's ropes—forget it. Leave that to professional daredevils who are getting paid for taking chances. You can really get hurt doing that!

33. Multiple skiing: These Bantam Lake Ski Clubbers are practicing a show routine on trick skis.

CHAPTER SIX

Slalom

"Slalom" is a Norwegian term meaning: "Skiing, usually in a race against time, in a zigzag downhill course." This snow skiing definition is also appropriate for water skiing—except, of course, for the word "downhill."

34. Slalom: The late Joe Cash at Callaway Gardens sending up a tremendous wall of water during a cut in his slalom run. I consider Cash to have been one of the greatest over-all skiers ever. (Courtesy American Ski Association)

To most people slalom water skiing is merely cutting back and forth across the wake on one ski. Many think it is a contest to see how hard you can cut on a single ski so that your shoulder almost touches the water. If you can hang on through such a cut, your ski sends up an impressive wall of spray which makes slalom skiing exciting for both skier and spectators. But there is more to good slalom than just a strong back and arms. There is technique! Let's start from the beginning—with the ski.

Almost any ski out of a pair of standard skis can be skied on alone, should you kick off or lose the other. But for optimum control, speed, and performance, a specially designed slalom ski is necessary.

The most proven, functional design today is the banana type with the bullet-shaped tip and tapering tail. Some slalom skis taper from 6½ to seven inches wide at the front binder to two inches at the tail. All slalom skis have a deep, knifelike tail fin or keel for stabilization.

Naturally, since both feet are placed on the same ski, the binders are mounted in line, the front binder usually placed to locate the skier's ankle bone over the center of the ski. The "rear binder" is usually just a toepiece into which the rear foot is slipped after the skier has gotten up. Non-skid tape under the rear binder prevents that foot from slipping on the ski, since this type of rear binder doesn't keep your heel from sliding sideways. A few slalom skiers prefer a rear binder heelpiece, but it is difficult to get your foot into this kind of rear binder when skiing, so they start out from either the water or a dock with both feet already in the binders—which is harder to do than what you are about to learn.

The latest slalom ski design utilizes a one-quarter inch to one-half inch quarter-round or bevel all the way around the bottom edge. This bevel causes suction at the tail which keeps the ski from popping out of the water at very high speeds and helps the skier decelerate after a cut. Deceleration (or braking) is just as important in negotiating a slalom course as acceleration.

Several years ago, the "concave" hit the scene. A slight hollow was milled into the bottom of the slalom ski. This development was premised somewhat on the snow ski groove theory—to make

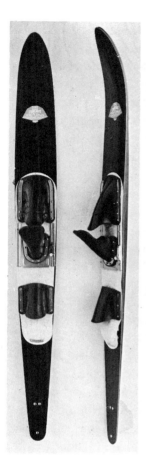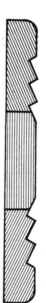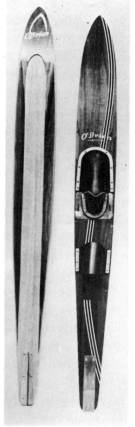

Slalom skis:

35. *Left:* Top and side view of a concave slalom: Note the comfortable cushion under the binders. Ski has melamine top and bottom surfaces which offer great speed and low maintenance. The binder is adjustable. (Courtesy Superior Sports Specialties)

36. *Center:* A grooved slalom: Counter angle grooves are milled into the bottom. (See cross section drawing.) Ski has a fixed binder. (Courtesy Cypress Gardens Skis)

37. *Right:* Bottom and top view of a competition slalom: bottom view shows how concave is milled into bottom of ski. Note how fin is attached to ski via slot in tail and reinforcing top plate. Binders are mounted slightly farther forward on this ski. (Courtesy O'Brien Skis)

it track better. Concaves did track better, but many skiers found they couldn't "hook" them (make sudden, very sharp cuts) as well. Most slalom competitors, however, felt that the end result was beneficial, because the "hooker" is more than likely to get clobbered when he falls behind on the slalom course, while the "technician," who skis a steady, acceleration-deceleration method, usually takes the honors. So the concave is here to stay, and almost every big-name slalom skier in the country uses one.

Still, not all slalom buffs were satisfied. In early 1967 another concept appeared: the grooved slalom. Counter-angle grooves were milled into the bottom full length of the ski—three on each side of a flat center. Advocates of the grooved slalom rate it superior to the concave because the grooves are nearer the ski's edges, while by necessity a concave can only be milled in the center. Since during a cut the ski is literally banked on its edge, the grooves are supposedly brought into play more efficiently.

Which design is best will be proven in future years. Of course, some skiers will always be partial to what they're accustomed to, and understandably so; why should they chuck a good old ski that they can "make talk" just to keep up with the Joneses?

Remember, it takes a while to get used to anything new. So if you're disappointed with a new design after riding it the first time, don't draw any rash conclusions. Give it a chance. It may take you five or ten rides. Use the following table as a guide in choosing a ski:

RECOMMENDED SIZES FOR SLALOM SKIS

Skier's Weight	Recommended Sizes*	
	Length of Ski	Width of Ski**
50–100 lbs.	56″–60″	5½″–6½″
100–150 lbs.	60″–66″	6½″
150–250 lbs.	66″–70″	6½″–7″

* At ordinary speeds of 25 to 36 mph.
** At maximum width.

SKIER'S SALUTE:

Success Factor: 1 to 5 tries

The first step in learning to ride one ski is to practice the skier's salute. Using standard skis, try this trick at twenty to twenty-two miles per hour. Skiing directly behind the boat, slowly shift your weight to one ski, and gently lift the other ski off the water. Lift the tip higher than the tail so that it can't catch or dig in the water. Ride with this lifted (salute) ski just barely off the water for a while. If you should feel unsteady, just lower it back on the water, *tail first!*

When you feel yourself getting steadier, raise the tip of the "salute" ski higher. To make a proper "skier's salute," raise the tip of the lifted ski to a forty-five-degree angle, or more, by bringing your knee up tightly toward your chest.

Letting go with the salute-side hand and raising it makes the stunt look more graceful, more balletlike.

Some skiers ask, "Which foot should I ski on, and which foot should I raise?" To find out, try lifting first one ski and then the other. One way will feel steadier. From then on it will be your "slalom" or one-ski foot.

38. Skier's salute. Beth Peckinpaugh makes sure to keep the tip of her "salute" ski up so it won't catch in the water.

39, 40, 41. Kicking off one ski: Beth makes all movements slowly so as
not to lose her balance.

KICKING OFF ONE SKI:

Success Factor: 1 to 7 tries

The easiest way to ride on one ski is to get up on two standard skis and kick one off. Naturally, kick off the ski you picked up while doing the skier's salute. It now becomes the "kick-off" ski.

Before starting, loosen the kick-off ski's binder so that it will slip off easily. Get up in the usual manner and when skiing at a steady speed of twenty-two to twenty-four miles per hour with your skis one foot apart, slowly shift your weight to your slalom foot.

When 90 percent of your weight is on your slalom ski, slowly lift your heel almost out of the kick-off ski's binder, but keep your toes in the toe binder. Now almost 100 percent of your weight is on your slalom ski.

In a brisk, smooth motion, pull your toes out of the kick-off ski by bending your knee back. The kick-off ski will trail off to your rear. You are now riding on one ski, so if you feel shaky, you may *lightly* drag the toes of your free foot in the water to steady your-self. Then slowly, gingerly, place your free foot on the ski behind the other and gradually divide your weight equally on each foot. Making all movements or weight changes gradually avoids lots of spills. Try to relax as much as possible.

After three or four rides, substitute a slalom ski for one of the standard skis, and kick off the remaining standard ski. This way you'll get practice slipping your rear foot into a binder. At first you'll probably shove it in only part of the way, but you'll soon learn how to kick into the rear binder securely.

To turn or steer the ski, simply lean one way or the other, shifting some of your weight to your rear foot, which should be flat on the ski. Stay inside the wake until you feel confident. When crossing the wake, do it with some momentum so that you'll drift twenty to thirty feet outside the wake; then "slalom" back in again. Lean gently at first; then gradually pull harder with each turn. Soon you'll be cutting. Remember, there's no substitute for prac-tice. Spend lots of time on that slalom ski!

42, 43, 44. Crossing the wake: Lean gently, but cross the wake with definite momentum.

GETTING UP ON ONE SKI FROM THE WATER:

Success Factor: 1 to 5 tries

Wade out in waist-deep (or deeper) water and put on your slalom ski, with the binder snug. Pull your ski knee in close to your chest, keeping the ski tip out of the water.

Tell the driver "In gear" so you'll get the feel of being pulled slowly forward. Dragging your free foot directly behind you, with toes pointed aft, will help steady you.

Then yell "Hit it," and freeze, keeping only a slight bend in your arms. Use the baseball grip on the handle. Stay directly over the ski. The speed should be the same as if you were on two skis.

Don't try to stand up as the boat accelerates and the ski begins to surface. Keep your free foot dragging behind you until the ski is planing nicely. Then straighten up a bit and place your free foot in the rear binder. If you fall to either side during the start, it means that you're not staying directly over the ski. A spill forward over the tip indicates you're not low enough to compensate for the stronger pull needed to get up on one ski. Falling backward means you're "bracing" or leaning too much against the boat's pull.

Remember, freeze in that starting position, and don't make any unnecessary fast movements.

45, 46, 47, 48, 49. One-ski deep water start: Beth "freezes" in proper starting position until she's surfaced. Then she slowly places her free foot on the back of the ski.

One-ski jump start off the dock: For this start your driver must accelerate quickly. Some skiers even take in slack rope to give the boat a head start, but this could result in a violent jerk and may throw the skier forward on his nose.

50. As the line tightens, Scotty steps off the dock.

51. His ski sinks slightly into the water, but his forward speed quickly planes it.

52. It begins to surface again . . .

53. . . . and he rides away.

WAKE JUMPING ON A SLALOM SKI:

Success Factor: 1 to 3 tries

Become accustomed to your slalom ski before jumping the wake. The technique is the same as with two skis except the landings are more critical, and constant control is essential. Your boat speed should be between twenty-six and thirty-six miles per hour.

Start with small hops at moderate speeds. As you gain confidence, begin cutting toward the wake to accelerate before hitting it. However, make sure of one thing: *Stop cutting before you meet the wake.* If you are still cutting as you jump off the wake, you're in for a tumble.

54. Buster McCalla does a spectacular one-ski wake jump. (Courtesy Cypress Gardens)

THE HARD CUT:

There's more to cutting hard than just leaning and pulling. Fine edge control, weight distribution, timing, and path selection must all be coordinated. To practice hard cuts, ski slowly outside the wake to a point about thirty-five to forty feet from its center, avoiding slack rope of any kind. As you are slowing down out there, bend slightly forward at the waist, placing more weight on your front foot. Hold the handle with your inside hand, and extend it toward the boat for better reach.

Begin the cut by pulling in on the handle, grasping it with both hands, and bring your upper torso back as you lean against the boat's momentum. Pull only to the first wake—then stop cutting and decelerate an equal distance to the other side, at which point you'll prepare to cut back.

CUTTING AROUND A SLALOM BUOY:

After you've mastered the hard cut, you can test your control by setting out a buoy (any old plastic bottle or beach ball tied to an anchor will do) and practice cutting around it. Ask the driver to pass it holding a straight line about thirty-five to forty feet from it. Try to make a sharp circular "cut" around the buoy, getting as close to the downcourse side of the buoy as possible.

The trick is to approach the buoy wide, while still decelerating, with no slack rope, and *actually begin the turn before you reach the buoy,* so that as you brush by it on the downcourse side you're already heading toward the wake. (If, when you're even with the buoy, your path is parallel with that of the boat, or heading away from the wake, you're beginning your turn too late.) Don't favor one side. Practice cutting both right and left around a buoy. Of course, your driver will have to drive accordingly.

HOW TO PRACTICE RHYTHMIC SLALOM SKIING WITHOUT AN OFFICIAL COURSE:

Practice behind a fast, powerful boat at increasing speeds, but start off at a comfortable twenty-two to twenty-six miles per hour, depending on your size and weight. Having told your driver always to drive straight and at a steady speed, ski out about forty feet from the center of the wake and make a strong cut. Stop pulling at the first wake, and begin deceleration so that your forward momentum is spent about forty feet on the other side of the wake. Then cut back again, and so on.

If slack rope appears, you're cutting back prematurely. Remember, when cutting pull the handle in toward your waist and never cut past the first wake. Upon decelerating, bend forward at the waist to switch your weight slightly forward. Always stay within forty feet of the center of the wake.

Skiing the slalom course:

55. Wayne Grimditch approaches the course from its far left and begins his cut toward the entrance gate.

56. As he goes through, he eases his cut.

57. His momentum carries him to the far right, well before Buoy 1, and he begins a gradual decelerating bank.

58. Starting his cut well before reaching the buoy, he grazes it on the downcourse side.

59. He cuts hard . . .

60. . . . but stops his cut as he reaches the wake . . .

61. . . . thereby switching his edge and beginning his decelerative approach arc for Buoy 2.

62. He begins another powerful cut well before that buoy. And, hopefully, he'll continue down the course and out the end gate.

THE SLALOM COURSE AND HOW TO NEGOTIATE IT:

If you now have a strong cut, can jump wakes, and feel at home on your slalom ski, timing and technique are the only additional essentials to running an official slalom course.

An official slalom course is composed of twenty-two buoys laid out as prescribed by the American Water Ski Association. There are eight pairs of boat gates laid out in a straight line as shown in Diagram D. The boat has to be driven in a straight line between these eight pairs of buoys. On each side of the boat path, evenly and alternately spaced, are six slalom buoys around which the skier must turn while the boat is driven in a straight line through the boat gates. These slalom buoys are located 12½ yards from the boat path.

The great slalom champion, Warren Witherell, once said, "The most obvious, but often neglected fact about the slalom event is that it is a race. The skier who can maneuver a prescribed course

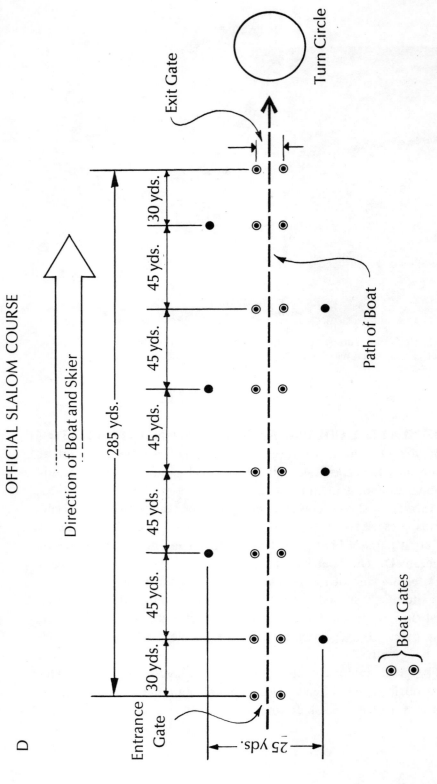

OFFICIAL SLALOM COURSE

Direction of Boat and Skier

285 yds.

30 yds. | 45 yds. | 45 yds. | 45 yds. | 45 yds. | 45 yds. | 30 yds.

Entrance Gate

25 yds.

Exit Gate

Turn Circle

Path of Boat

Boat Gates

Slalom Buoy

D

at the highest rate of speed is the winner." He mentioned further the ". . . need for great acceleration as close to each buoy as possible." If the slalom skier can do this at the first buoy, he can actually get a good head start on the course.

Begin practicing on the slalom course at twenty-four to twenty-six miles per hour using a seventy-five-foot rope, behind a boat possessing speed and pull power. Thirty-five- or fifty-horsepower outboards will fool you, since your cuts around each slalom buoy will slow the boat by three to five miles per hour. Then, should you have occasion to enter a tournament behind powerful tow-boats, you'll miss the second or third buoys.

Instruct your driver to guide the boat straight down the course without varying speed. First check him out through the course without a skier. He should be lined up with the boat gates at least 150 feet before entering the course and must hold a straight boat path for at least seventy-five feet after leaving it, so that he has plenty of room to make a "barbell" turn before entering the course in the opposite direction.

SKIING THE COURSE: (see Diagram E)

When slalom skiing, always wear some form of flotation, preferably a ski vest. Before entering the course swing out to the left, your eyes glued on the first gate. As the boat passes through the first boat gate, cut toward the gate. When you pass through the gate, stop cutting and begin deceleration to a point about fifteen feet before the first buoy, and eight to ten feet wide of it. *This will give you your head start.*

At that point cut hard to the left, brushing past the downcourse side of the buoy. During the cut from the buoy to the wake keep your body as straight as possible, with ankles, knees, hips, and neck in line, but don't worry about a slight bend forward at the waist. Pull hard only to the wake, then ease up and decelerate, preferably to a point ahead of and wide of Buoy 2 in order to get a head start on that buoy. As you decelerate crossing the wake, gradually extend your arms forward for full reach, finally releasing the outside arm for balance. Bending the upper torso forward

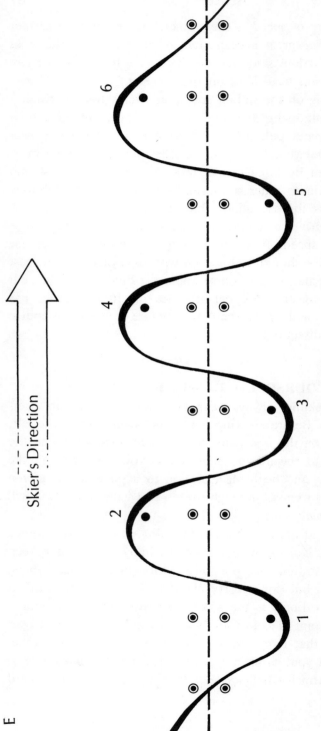

SKIING THE SLALOM COURSE

Skier's Direction

Skier Accelerating

Skier Decelerating

Path of Boat

Boat Gates

Slalom Buoy

leaves you in good position to take up slack rope when you begin turning for the buoy. Make believe the buoy is closer to you and wider out than it really is, and begin your cuts before actually passing the buoy. *Otherwise you'll be later and later at each successive buoy, finally missing one.* Repeat this technique for the next four buoys, making sure to pass through the final boat gate.

That's all there is to it. Practice at one speed until you've rounded all the buoys. Then increase boat speed in two-mile-per-hour increments.

Concentrate on keeping pressure on the rope during each turn, pulling hard to the wake. Warren Witherell says: "I am convinced that it is more important to turn on a tight line than it is to turn sharply." This is borne out by the fact that many female slalom artists succeed in making very difficult slalom course runs. They have the technique of keeping the rope taut and skiing around each buoy as efficiently as possible. They are not as strong as men and do not cut as hard, yet they are exceptional in slalom.

Your free hand should always grasp the handle quickly after beginning the turn so that both arms can "pull," using the baseball-bat grip.

A good check on your slalom technique is to have your observer watch which side of your ski is emitting spray. For instance, in correctly traveling from Buoy 1 to Buoy 2, the spray will come off the right edge of your ski until you meet the wake. Then as deceleration begins after crossing the wake, spray will come off the ski's left edge, signaling the beginning of the next (right) turn. Remember, hook turns shouldn't be used except when you are extremely late for the last buoy. A more gradual power turn is preferable and more easily controllable.

In competition, slalom speeds vary from twenty-four to thirty-six miles per hour. Local tournaments usually start at twenty-four to twenty-eight miles per hour, depending upon the division. On each subsequent pass, the boat speed is raised two miles per hour. After attaining top speed (thirty-six miles per hour for men's and boy's divisions; thirty-four miles per hour for all other divisions), the rope is first shortened twelve feet; then it is further shortened in six-foot increments until all competitors are eliminated. The skier who negotiates the most consecutive buoys, wins. If there is a tie, the skier scoring the most total buoys wins. If that is also tied, a "sudden death" runoff is held between the tied skiers, starting at one speed increment below the one they both missed.

Technique is most important, but brute strength can be helpful. Do a lot of practice slalom skiing outside the course, in all kinds of water, rough or smooth, cutting hard and jumping the wake. Begin your slalom course practice at or above the highest speed you have previously mastered, but several days before a tournament go back to the scheduled starting speed and work up. Don't practice the day before competition. The lay-off will freshen both your body and technique.

A stopwatch is necessary to keep an accurate check on boat speed, by timing the number of seconds it takes the boat to pass through the slalom course. This is an interesting job for your observer, but there is a knack to it, so check him out first. He must start the stopwatch as the boat passes through the entrance gate, and stop it as the boat passes out the end gate. The official times and speeds are as follows:

OFFICIAL SLALOM TIMES AND SPEEDS

Miles Per Hour	Actual Time in Seconds
22	26.5
24	24.3
26	22.4
28	20.8
30	19.4
32	18.2
34	17.1
36	16.2

ACTUAL SKIER'S SPEED:

What speeds does the skier himself attain on a slalom course? Well, the skier travels 19 percent farther than the boat. While the boat is traveling at a steady speed of thirty-six miles per hour, the skier averages 42.8 miles per hour. The skier, however, accelerates and decelerates so that in the straightaway between the buoys he peaks out at around fifty miles per hour.

AN EASY, INEXPENSIVE WAY TO LAY OUT A SLALOM COURSE:

There are several ways to lay out a slalom course. If you live in the northern half of the nation, it's easiest to wait until the ice forms. Then two persons can easily lay out a course with a tape measure, cut holes in the ice and drop in anchors and underwater floats with plumb-bob accuracy. Then, in late spring the buoys can be attached.

The following is probably the simplest, most inexpensive way to set out a slalom course in the water. If the instructions are followed carefully, it will be satisfactorily accurate.

MATERIALS:

22 anchors:

> Seventy-five to one-hundred pounders which can be made up of two large concrete blocks, or a three-gallon pail of cement or heavy old cast-iron parts.

22 buoys:

> Large airtight plastic bottles (such as empty one-gallon bleach bottles).

22 underwater floats:

> Small styrofoam blocks (6 inches square) or one-quart airtight plastic bottles. These enable you to find the anchor rope easily should a buoy break loose.

Anchor rope:

> One-quarter-inch nylon or polyethylene. Multiply the depth of the water by twenty-two to compute the quantity needed, then add 5 percent for good measure.

22 elastic strips:

> One-quarter-inch shock cord or strips cut from truck tire tubes each five to six feet long by one inch wide. These keep proper tension on buoys, should the water level change slightly. They also dampen the strain on the anchor line and anchors.

MEASURING LINE

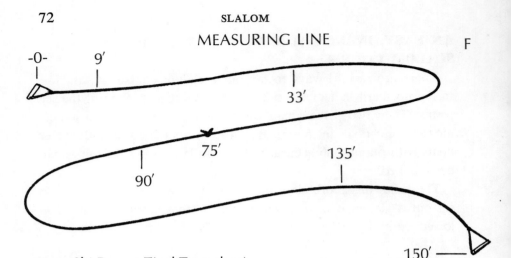

(Two Ski Ropes Tied Together)

MEASURING LINES:

Two seventy-five-foot ski ropes tied together make excellent measuring lines. Measuring from one end, put a piece of tape or other suitable mark at nine feet, thirty-three feet, ninety feet, and 135 feet. (See Diagram F.)

MEN AND EQUIPMENT:

Three strong (and patient) swimmers wearing life preservers and/or wet suits are advisable. Swim fins help a lot in swimming from one point to the other.

Use two boats to carry tools, anchors, ropes, floats, and swimmers to the proposed site. Attach small floats to knives and scissors to prevent loss.

PREPARING THE ANCHORS:

First spot-check the slalom course site with a lightweight anchor and rope to learn the water depth.

Estimating the length of each anchor rope, tie together the anchor, line, underwater float, and rubber strip. Then loosely fasten a plastic bottle to the high end of the elastic strip so that it can be untied and readjusted for depth and tension after the anchor has been dropped. (See Diagram G.)

TYPICAL SLALOM BUOY

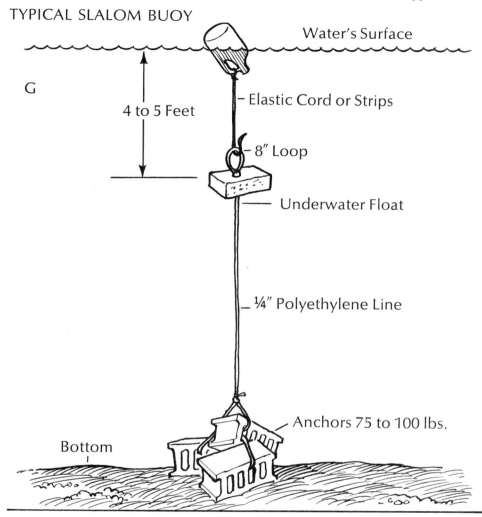

Water's Surface

G

4 to 5 Feet

- Elastic Cord or Strips

8" Loop

Underwater Float

¼" Polyethylene Line

Anchors 75 to 100 lbs.

Bottom

SETTING THE ANCHORS:

Lay out the course when the water is glassy calm. Otherwise the job will be next to impossible. Two swimmers should stretch the measuring rope to find the proper spot for each successive buoy. While these swimmers hold the rope tight, the boat should slowly idle over to the proper mark and stop, so that an anchor can be lowered down gently at the mark. It will rarely be accurate at the initial dropping. A third swimmer should then take up any slack in the anchor line by shortening the rubber strip, until one-fourth of the buoy is submerged. The swimmers should then recheck with the measuring line for proper positioning and shift the anchor to the correct point, if necessary. This procedure must be followed with each anchor to obtain an accurate course. Be sure to use the same tension on the measuring line, when stretching it for each measurement.

THREE EASY STEPS TO LAY OUT A SLALOM COURSE

H

STEP 1

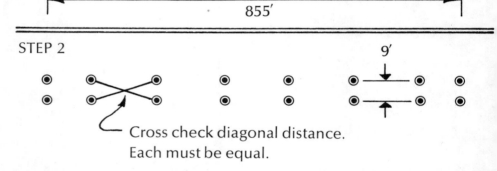

STEP 2

Cross check diagonal distance.
Each must be equal.

STEP 3

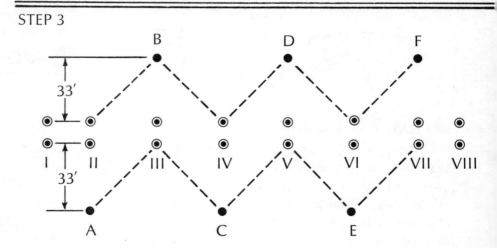

LAYING OUT THE COURSE: (See Diagram H)

Step 1. Set out eight buoys in a perfectly straight line, the prescribed distances apart. They should form a line 855 feet long.

Step 2. Set out eight more buoys exactly nine feet away from the first row. Each buoy in the second row should be exactly across from its counterpart in the first row. Cross checking the diagonal distances between each rectangle formed by four buoys is a good way to insure accuracy. They must be equal.

Step 3. Sighting across Gates II, III, IV, V, VI, and VII, set out Buoys A, B, C, D, E, and F, respectively.

At this stage the course will be usable, but the buoys should be double-checked by measuring the buoy-gate distances as shown in the dotted lines in Step 3 (see Diagram H). Each should be 139 feet. This final double-check will probably take your swimmers an extra hour, but it is worth it.

If you live in a problem area having very deep water, moving currents, or other geographical limitations, write the American Water Ski Association for its very fine booklet, *How to Lay Out a Slalom Course*. Official slalom buoys are also available from the AWSA.

63. Cypress Gardens skiers perform a tricky "over and under." (Courtesy Cypress Gardens)

CHAPTER SEVEN

Jumping

Jumping is by far the most exciting event in water skiing. That's why water ski jumpers are known to the general public as the daredevils of the sport. Even so, skiers of all ages can learn to jump. Sure, you can take a good hard spill off the ramp, but who says you can't take a fall that smarts off a fast slalom ski? Let's face it, in almost any sport you take your black-and-blues, and ski jumping can give you an incomparable thrill and a sense of mastery that relatively few people experience during their lifetimes.

Pursue it intelligently, keeping in mind technique and safety, and by all means have the patience to learn gradually. In other words, learn well!

THE RAMP:

Use only an AWSA regulation jumping ramp. There's a reason for every bolt and board in the regulation ramp, so if you plan on building one, write AWSA headquarters for a complete blueprint.

The ramp surface exposed to the skier is twenty-two feet long by fourteen feet wide. Its height at the takeoff end can usually be adjusted from three to six feet. The recommended ramp surface is three-quarter-inch marine plywood, sanded smooth and waxed with a special formula of carnauba and paraffin (also available from the AWSA).

One good wax application is generally sufficient to last three to four months of average ramp usage.

All good jumping ramps have protective sides which slant downward from the ramp surface into the water. Since many ski jumpers cut toward the ramp at a very sharp side angle, these "side curtains" prevent the possibility of a skier careening into the ramp's inner construction timbers, and fend him off, usually unhurt.

Many ski clubs build their own ramps. Materials alone cost anywhere from five hundred to one thousand dollars. Usually a ski club negotiates with a local lumber dealer to furnish the materials for nothing (or cost) in return for the club allowing him to advertise his products tastefully on the ramp's sides, which make fine "billboards." If you can afford the ramp without concessions, the sides make a convenient place for the club name and insignia.

Many modern ramps contain a pumping device which sprays a continuous stream of water on the surface, keeping the wax hard and "fast" when the ramp is in use. Small gasoline engines (similar to lawn mower motors) are used for this purpose, but these frequently break down, need constant refueling, and are often hard to start. Becoming popular now is a small submersible pump driven by an electric battery. A twelve-volt mobile battery can power such a pump for many hours before recharging is necessary—if the skiers are prudent and turn the pump on just before they jump, shutting it off promptly when they are finished.

The ramp should be sturdy and should be constructed of good-quality materials. Always inspect it before jumping to make sure that there are no rough spots, protruding nails, or slivers, and that the waxed surface is wet. If you don't have a pumping system, wet the surface down well with half a dozen pailsful of water before you jump.

JUMPING SKIS:

Jumping without proper skis can prove dangerous to the skier and damaging to ordinary skis and to the ramp's surface. Skis need extra reinforcement and special resilience to withstand the terrific shocks inflicted by jumping. Although banana shapes have been tried, the most successful design in jumping skis is the "square back": much like standard skis, sixty-eight inches long by 6½

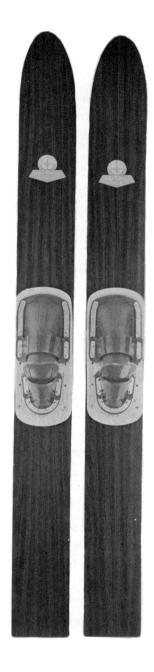
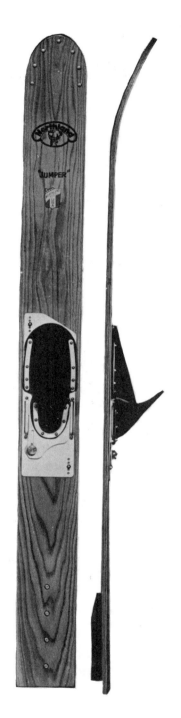

64, 65. Two types of jumping skis.

    Left: Both tops and bottoms of the jumpers have slick melamine surfaces. Note carpetlike control cushions under binders to lessen shock. (Courtesy 3S Company)

    Right: Jumpers made of laminated ash. Note custom plate binders. (Courtesy Northland Ski Manufacturing Co.)

inches wide, and anywhere from one-half to three-quarters of an inch thick. Skiers under one hundred pounds should use a sixty-inch length. Naturally, the better your binders, the better you'll jump. Most ski jumpers paste a one-half-inch rubber heel pad inside the binders to cushion the shock of landings.

Each jumping ski has a single one-half-inch-wide hardwood or plastic keel or skeg (sharp metal fins cannot be used), which should be checked occasionally for proper attachment and smoothness. Screws projecting from the bottoms of your jumping skis can throw you for a dangerous spill on the ramp and/or scratch up the expensive ramp surface very badly. Keep a good, hard marine finish on your skis, topped by a coat of car wax.

WHERE TO DRIVE THE BOAT:

Ninety-nine out of every hundred water ski jumpers approach the ramp from the right—that is, the boat passes to the right of the ramp and the skier cuts to his left to go off the ramp. A few ski jumpers still jump "Texas style," from the other side.

Recently there has been a drive to completely eliminate left-side jumping, since many AWSA tournament sites do not have sufficient room on both sides of the ramp. For this reason jumping should only be learned as specified in this book—from the right.

DRIVING FOR SKI JUMPERS:

The most important point for the driver to remember is always to drive the boat in a straight line and parallel to the right edge of the ramp surface (not parallel to the sloping protective side, which is often flared out at an angle). Once the skier begins his approach to the ramp, the driver should hold the designated boat speed steady until five or six seconds after the skier's landing. If the skier falls, the driver should return to him quickly and safely (without running the fallen skier down!). Many overanxious drivers, thinking the skier may be shaken up, whip the boat back to the skier at dangerously high speeds, almost out of control, putting the fallen skier in jeopardy.

If you have trouble estimating a path parallel to the ramp, make sure you don't turn "in" (or left) on the skier. This will cause slack in the rope. Rather, turn "out" or right very slightly after passing the ramp, to make sure the skier keeps a tight rope.

In order to insure calm water in the ramp's vicinity, always drive the barbell course pattern as shown in Diagram I.

Naturally, *always have an observer in the boat* when towing a ski jumper. He should watch the skier, keep you posted as to what is happening, and relay the skier's signals.

Be aware of your function; that is, to drive accurately and safely for the ski jumper. Make sure that the observer watches the jumper constantly. The observer is not there to joyride, or make conversation, or entertain the driver. You'd be surprised how often this happens.

66. Wayne Grimditch ready to go jumping. Note his ski vest and helmet.

PREPARATION FOR YOUR FIRST JUMP:

Lower the ramp to its lowest height; anywhere between three and five feet is fine. A four-foot rise in twenty-two feet is really a very flat ascending angle of about 10½ degrees. You'll feel little jolt or bump as you slide up the ramp.

Wear a life vest or "jump jacket" that provides ample flotation. Many ski jumpers also wear wet suits of three-sixteenths-inch neoprene, which soften the hard knocks of a spill, and also provide extra flotation. Pick a calm, sunny day for your first jumping experience, and choose the best boat driver you can find, definitely one who has driven for jumpers. Before going over the ramp, familiarize yourself with your jumping skis. Slalom back and forth and jump the wake several times to learn how they feel when landing. At first your boat speed should be twenty-two to twenty-four miles per hour. Tell the driver to drive thirty feet to the right of the ramp and parallel to it. He should give you a long, straight course, at least one hundred yards before and after the ramp.

YOUR FIRST JUMP:

Success Factor: 1 to 2 tries

Many skiers who would love to try jumping can't seem to get by the psychological barrier of going off "that big thing" the first

67, 68, 69. Your first jump: Path 1.

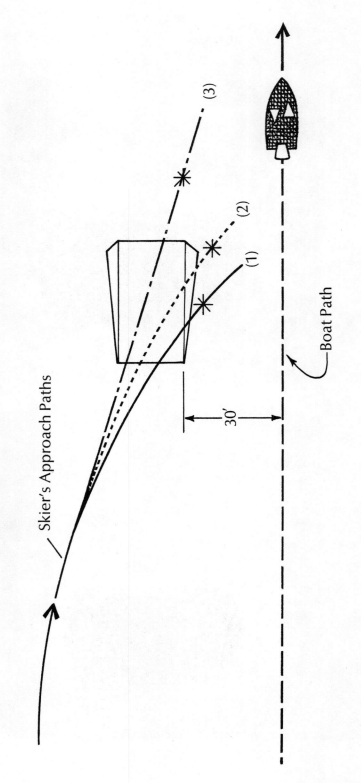

GRADUALLY WORKING UP TO YOUR FIRST JUMP

Skier's Approach Paths

(1)

(2)

(3)

30'

Boat Path

 Landing

time. This is understandable, but there is a very simple, gradual way you can work up to your first jump. Simply don't go off the whole ramp. All you need do at first is to go off a portion of the ramp: the bottom corner! (See Diagram I.)

Following Path 1 as the boat makes its pass toward the ramp, ski far outside the *left wake* in a low, vertical crouch and line yourself up as if you were planning to ski past the *left side* of the ramp. About seventy-five feet from the ramp, drift toward the right corner, aiming for a point about three feet in from the right edge of the ramp. This angle (Skier's Path 1) will cause you to leave the *side* of the ramp at a height of only one or two feet above the water's surface, making a very gradual first jump.

After a couple of break-in jumps, try going off the ramp a little higher, as shown in Path 2. Plan your path accurately. Just before you reach the ramp, freeze and allow the boat to pull you naturally across the ramp. When leaving the ramp, stay low and rigid, with your weight directly over your binders. Keep your knees bent and your head up. Your eyes should be looking directly forward. Grasp the towbar in the baseball-bat grip, keeping

70, 71, 72. Path 2.

your arms almost straight, and hold onto the handle with both hands throughout the jump.

After successfully completing Path 2, proceed to the full jump, Path 3. Aim for the ramp to meet it just inside the left corner. Since you should approach it in a gradual drift to the right, your path up the ramp will be diagonal, as shown. Just before ascending the ramp, plant your weight on the balls of your feet, squarely over your skis, which should be about a foot apart. Skiing on the ramp surface will feel more slippery than skiing on water. Once on the ramp, don't try to turn or cut. Skis just don't track on waxed, wet marine plywood.

When you leave the ramp, always try to keep your skis parallel, tips up. Novice ski jumpers should hold the vertical crouch position from approach to landing. Waving your arms or legs could easily throw you off balance. Hold the handle out in front of you, arms almost straight at about waist height. Look at the horizon, not down at the water.

The impact on landing from a four- or five-foot ramp is similar to jumping off a table. "Give" only slightly in your knees when you land so that you won't have a tendency to sit back in the water. Practice Path 3 until you succeed every time. "Fanny dunking" or "bottoming" can be avoided by bending forward at the waist (weight on the balls of your feet) before you ascend the ramp and holding that position throughout the jump.

Falls are inevitable in water ski jumping, but injuries seldom occur if the sport is handled with respect and caution. After each fall, clasp both hands over your head in the standard "okay" signal.

A three- or four-foot ramp height will soon seem easy and may lose its challenge. If so, raise the ramp to five feet, which is the official jumping height for all divisions except the men's division (men seventeen to thirty-four years old jump at six). Naturally, novice men jumpers should practice at five feet before trying the formidable six-foot height.

73, 74, 75, 76. Path 3.

THE SINGLE CUT

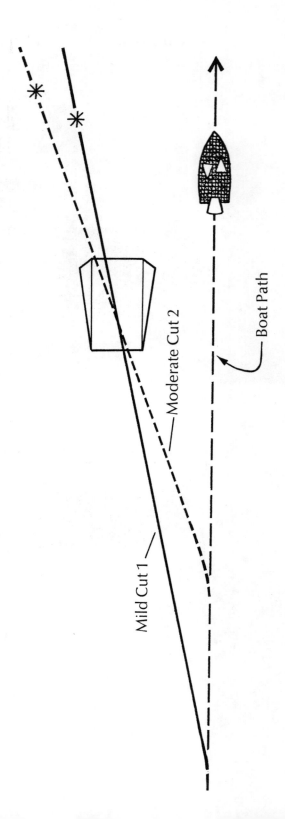

Mild Cut 1

Moderate Cut 2

Boat Path

✳ Landing

YOUR NEXT STEP—THE SINGLE CUT:

Assuming you've taken fifteen to fifty jumps, begin practicing the single cut. As before, have the boat pass twenty feet from the side of the ramp at a speed of about twenty-five miles per hour.

Two types of single cuts are shown in Diagram J. Practice the mild cut first. Skiing directly behind the boat, wait until you're about a hundred feet from the ramp, then start heading for the center of the ramp. At first you'll have to lean slightly to maintain your approach path, but as you draw nearer the ramp your speed will increase and you'll have to pull gently to meet the center of the ramp. Freeze in a low, vertical crouch and *stop leaning or pulling just before you ascend the ramp.* Follow all previous directions regarding in-air and landing techniques.

Gradually work up to the moderate cut. Basically it is the same, except that you begin the cut later, thereby increasing the angle at which you approach the ramp, so plan to meet the ramp four or five feet inside the right approach corner. The longer you wait before beginning the cut, the faster you'll hit the ramp. Freeze just before reaching the ramp, and hold that position through the jump and landing. By this time your jumping distances could be *increased by as much as thirty feet* over when you first started.

THE POP (OR SPRING OFF THE RAMP): (Diagram L)

It is now time to begin shaping up some basic jumping technique and style, which, of course, make for a longer and better jump.

The pop is a controlled spring or hop executed by the skier off the top of the ramp to give him more height and distance. Timing and direction are crucial factors. Popping in the wrong direction, too soon (at the bottom of the ramp) or too late (after becoming airborne) proves useless.

Begin practicing your pop after you have mastered the moderate single cut. Pop gently at first with a slight straightening of the knees. Time it so that the pop pushes you upward and forward just as you leave the lip of the ramp; this is the real secret of

77, 78, 79, 80. The mild single cut.

81, 82, 83, 84. The moderate single cut.

achieving a maximum pop. Your pop will be most effective if you react off the highest point of the ramp, but since you are on the ramp only a fraction of a second, your pop must begin earlier. The main rising force should take effect against the last (highest) part of the ramp.

After a few gentle pops, begin increasing the force of your pop. Remember to pop *forward*. Snapping your head and shoulders back, or perpendicular to the ramp's surface (see Diagram K, top) can actually shorten your jump. Always lean forward on the balls of your feet (a very stable position) and take advantage of the lift afforded by the incline of the ramp. Keep your shoulders well ahead of your hips and knees, as if you were climbing a steep hill. (See Diagram K, bottom.)

You may hold onto the handle with both hands in flight (a relatively new technique), but most jumpers let go with their outside (left) hand and clutch their left thigh or knee. By necessity this bends you forward at the waist.

At this point you are developing into a good "pleasure jumper," and you are probably thinking of making longer jumps and entering competition. You can increase your distance somewhat and eliminate slack rope by having the boat driven farther from the ramp. Most tournament skiers use a boat-ramp distance of thirty-five to forty feet. As you become more skillful, gradually work up to the regulation speeds set by the AWSA in tournament competition, which, according to age, are as follows:

AWSA REGULATION JUMPING SPEEDS

Division	Skiers' Age Limit	Boat Speed for Jumping—MPH
Men	17–34	35
Women	17–29	28
Senior Men	35 and over	28
Senior Women	30 and over	28
Boys	13–16	28
Girls	13–16	28
Junior Boys	12 and under	26
Junior Girls	12 and under	26

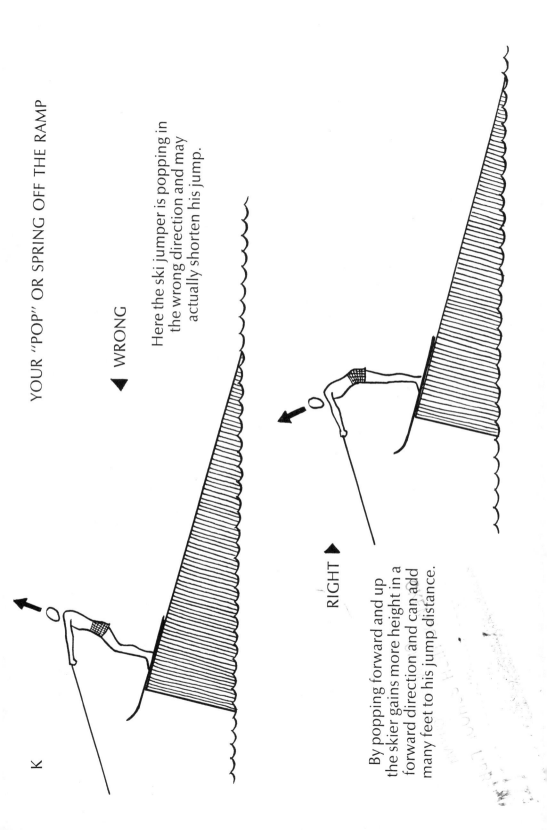

YOUR "POP" OR SPRING OFF THE RAMP

▲ WRONG

Here the ski jumper is popping in the wrong direction and may actually shorten his jump.

RIGHT ▲

By popping forward and up the skier gains more height in a forward direction and can add many feet to his jump distance.

K

THE DOUBLE WAKE CUT:

This technique is used to achieve maximum jumping distance. Learn it gradually and carefully. A split-second error in judgment making the skier late for the ramp can cause him to crash into the side of the ramp. The double wake cut should only be tried by experienced jumpers who have practiced the single wake cut, at their maximum recommended AWSA jumping speed, and have at least one hundred successful jumps to their credit.

First instruct your driver to give you a longer approach to the ramp—no less than 250 to three hundred yards. To aid him in judging proper boat-ramp distance, set out a buoy forty-five feet from the center of the ramp (see Diagram L) and tell him to drive just "inside the ball," which will position the boat path about thirty-three feet from the *side* of the ramp.

First use the mild double cut. On the approach, drift outside the right wake about thirty or forty feet. Just before the boat passes between you and the ramp, gradually begin your cut, aiming for the center of the ramp. As you start the cut, concentrate on one thing: holding a straight path from where you start your cut to the center of the ramp. In order to achieve this, you will have to pull harder and harder as you near the ramp. This type of cut is called the "progressive cut" because the skier actually accelerates all the way—a very important factor in obtaining maximum distance.

Increase your cuts gradually. The longer you wait before starting the cut, the harder and faster you'll have to pull to make the ramp.

Many double-cutters cut hard until they cross the second wake, then let up and glide, decelerating the rest of the way (see Diagram M). They would have gone farther had they skied straight up the ramp. Decelerating up the ramp will get you nothing— except the world's shortest jump. The best cut is one that enables you to ascend the ramp at the highest *controllable* speed. Many skiers can attain blinding speed by just cutting with all their might and hanging on. But can they handle the ramp at the end of such a "hairy" cut? No, sir. Eggbeatersville—that's where they're going.

The double wake cut:

85. Wayne begins his cut . . .

86. . . . cuts hard across the wake . . .

87. . . . stops cutting and stiffens his legs as he enters the transition zone just before the ramp . . .

88. . . . pops off the ramp . . .

89. . . . and leans forward for the sake of form and to keep his weight over his binders . . .

90. . . . to prepare for a solid landing.

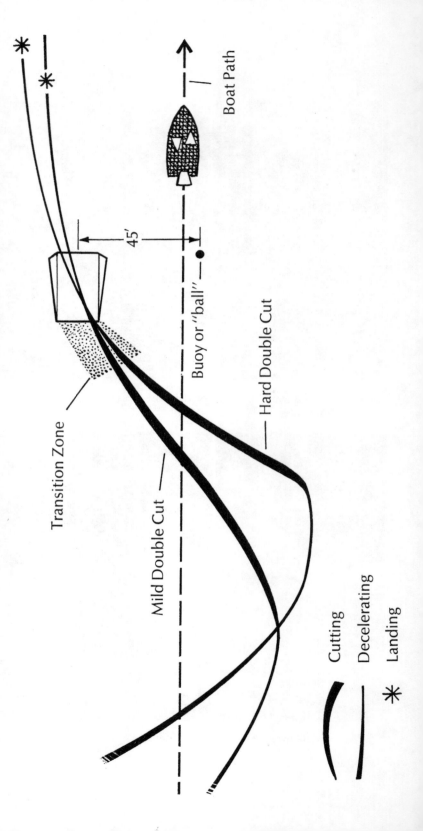

THE DOUBLE CUT

Boat Path

45'

Buoy or "ball"

Transition Zone

Hard Double Cut

Mild Double Cut

Cutting

Decelerating

Landing

L

BAD DOUBLE CUT TIMING

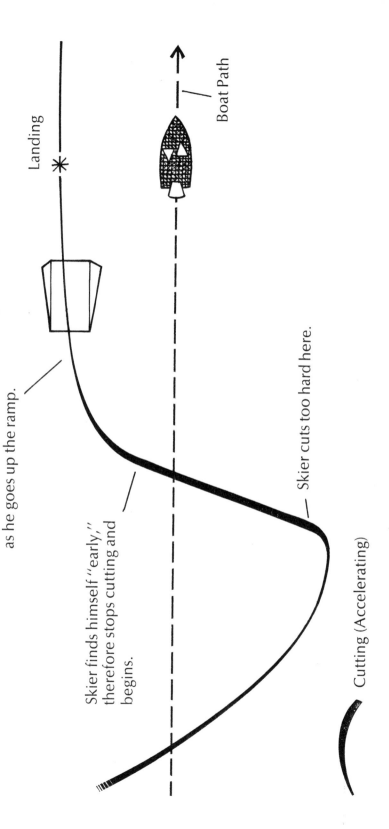

Landing

Boat Path

Skier continues to decelerate
as he goes up the ramp.

Skier finds himself "early,"
therefore stops cutting and
begins.

Skier cuts too hard here.

Cutting (Accelerating)

Start your cut gradually, pulling harder and harder until you enter the transition zone.

THE TRANSITION ZONE:

If you were to continue cutting right up to the ramp, your skis would slide out from under you, sending you for a bad spill. Why? Because you violated the transition zone (see Diagram M) —an area about fifteen feet before the base of the ramp where you *must end your cut to assume a stable jumping position.* Simply shift your weight from your heels to the balls of your feet and raise your hips. This movement executed just before ascending the ramp also forms the beginning of a beautiful forward pop.

ON THE RAMP (THE "CRUSH" FACTOR VS. THE POP):

Another problem that often befalls the jumper is "crushing" or collapsing on the ramp. This is caused by the abrupt ramp angle against which the jumper must react at high jumping speeds. What happens is that the skier's knees bend, forcing him to squat on the ramp. One common cause of crushing is that the skier's center of gravity is located too far behind his heels as he hits the ramp. He reacts quickly, trying to straighten his legs, but since his weight is too far back, this reaction merely forces the skis forward on the slippery surface, almost making him sit down on the ramp. Very often the jumper's skis are too far apart (farther than one foot). Reacting against the crush spreads them even farther, causing the skier's upper torso to pitch forward between them. The result may be a nasty spill. Had the skier made a proper transition before hitting the ramp, it could have been avoided.

When approaching the ramp at cutting speeds over forty miles per hour, you might find it advantageous to lock your knees as you reach the transition zone, but it is best to do this just after hitting the ramp, as a first stage of your pop. Make sure the main force of your pop is exerted in the last few feet before takeoff for maximum lift and distance.

THE FLIGHT:

The control you have during flight is almost wholly dependent on how well you negotiate your transition and pop. If you have a good solid "platform" while on the ramp, weight evenly distributed on both skis, and if you are propelled by the steadily accelerating force of a good progressive double cut, you will shoot off the ramp like a Jupiter Rocket. It won't be long before you develop your own style. Just remember to stay well forward, bent slightly at the waist, with your skis parallel, tips slightly higher than the tails. During flight, keep your head up, eyes on the horizon. Almost any form is considered correct if it is controlled and held constant throughout the jump's duration. Jerky actions, waving of arms or legs, and off-parallel skis can lower your form point totals. But your landing can really make or break you, from the point of view of form.

THE LANDING:

The AWSA Rule Book says: "Generally speaking, good form is that which permits a skier to obtain greatest distance while maintaining complete control over body and skis at all times." That part about maintaining "complete control over body and skis" applies to the landing, too, and landings aren't necessarily duck soup. If, during your flight, you maintain your weight directly over your skis, having popped off the ramp with the balls of your feet, and if you can land that way, you've got no problems.

A split second before landing, grasp the handle with both hands and stiffen your legs to prepare for the shock. Don't look down directly at the water, because you'll have a natural tendency to lean backward. Landing far to the left side of the boat path is final proof that your double cut was effective in that you have attained great speed.

HOW TO "BALK" SAFELY:

If, for any reason, during your double cut you find that you are late, don't hang on and try to make it! If you do, you'll crash into the side of the ramp. Balk!

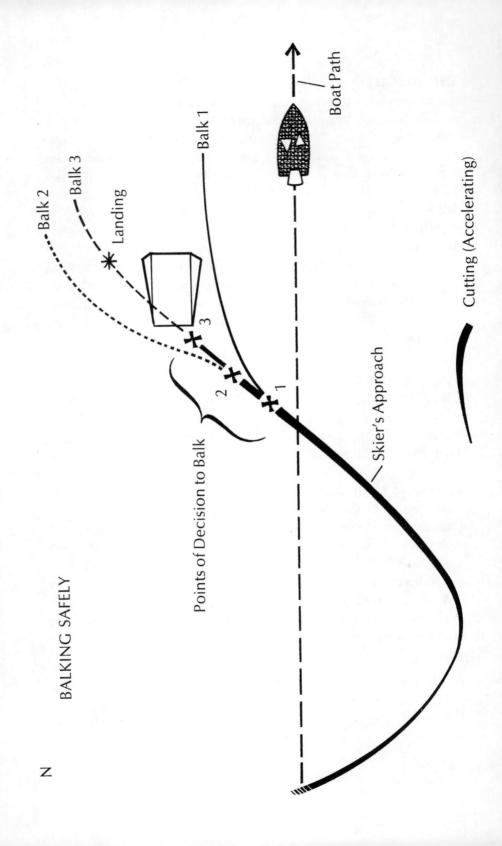

BALKING SAFELY

N

Boat Path

Balk 1

Balk 3

Balk 2

Landing

3

Points of Decision to Balk

2

1

Skier's Approach

Cutting (Accelerating)

Balking (see Diagram N) is deciding at the last moment to pass up the jump, but even that is tricky. A balk done incorrectly may not prevent you from colliding with the ramp. There are two ways to balk. One is to turn quickly and ski past the right side of the ramp (Balk 1). This method should only be used when the double cut hasn't reached "emergency status," usually before crossing the left wake.

The emergency balk must be used when you've already crossed the left wake. Instantly let go of the rope and "free-ski" to the *left* of the ramp (Balk 2). Often the jumper waits so long before letting go that he must ski over part of the approach end of the ramp and "free-jump" (Balk 3). This is scary but still safe; nevertheless, waiting that long is senseless and means taking unnecessary chances.

MEASURING HOW FAR YOU JUMP:

Once you begin "getting out there," you'll no doubt want to know how far you're jumping. A simple, inexpensive method is

Long-distance jumping. Wayne Grimditch at twenty-six miles per hour:

91. Wayne begins to let up on his cut as he enters the transition zone.

92. He stiffens his knees as he strikes the ramp . . .

93. . . . and pops hard, forward, and up.

94. In this jump he is using the new style of holding on with both hands.

95. About fifty feet out from the jump he is still rising as a result of his pop and great speed, so that he actually catches up with the towboat . . .

96, 97. . . . and lands almost directly to the left of the boat, for a jump of over one hundred feet.

to set out marker buoys at regular intervals, such as fifty, seventy-five, and one hundred feet. Station an observer either on shore opposite these markers, or in a boat a safe distance away. He can, within two or three feet, estimate how far you're jumping.

The American Water Ski Association uses the Johnson Sight Meter system, based on geometric and trigonometric principles. Two sighting stations are established on or near the shoreline. Each station is manned by two persons, each peering through a "sighting arm," which measures the angle from the jump to the point of the skier's landing. This information is then communicated to a pair of "plotters" who reconstruct the angles on a large master plotting board with two master board arms (straight-edges). The arms will cross at some point on a distance grid. The reading at this point gives the distance, within one foot accuracy. Johnson Sight Meters may be obtained from the American Water Ski Association.

JUST HOW FAR DO THEY JUMP?:

In 1947 Charles R. Sligh, Jr., jumped forty-nine feet at the renowned Dixie Tournament to establish the first national jumping record. In 1954 Warren Witherell broke the one-hundred-foot mark. The most hotly contested years in men's jumping were no doubt 1955 to 1960, during which men like Butch Rosenberg (at 125 feet), Alan Bromberg (at 126 feet), the great Joe Cash (at 142 feet), Mike Osborn (at 142 feet), and Penny Baker (at 150 feet) were in their prime. Then in 1964 a seventeen-year-old Californian, Dennis Rahlves, made water skiing history at the Rocky Mountain Open with an astounding leap of 158 feet—more than three times the distance jumped by Sligh in 1947 (when Rahlves was only several months old).

NATIONAL JUMPING RECORDS

Jumper	Division	Distance	Year	Ramp Height and Boat Speed
Michael Suyderhoud	Men	160′	1969	6′ ramp at 35 mph
Liz Allan	Women	110′	1968	5′ ramp at 28 mph
Dr. Keith Sutton	Sr. Men	112′	1964	5′ ramp at 28 mph
Johnny Blackburn	Boys	125′	1968	5′ ramp at 28 mph
Linda Lee Leavengood	Girls	109′	1968	5′ ramp at 28 mph
Wayne Grimditch	Jr. Boys	102′	1968	5′ ramp at 26 mph
Linda Lee Leavengood	Jr. Girls	86′	1964	5′ ramp at 26 mph
Irma Campbell	Sr. Women	85′	1965	5′ ramp at 28 mph

Probably the most outstanding accomplishment above is Johnny Blackburn's fantastic 125-foot leap—that being only thirty-five feet short of the men's record—considering the fact that Blackburn jumped off a five-foot ramp, with a boat speed of only twenty-eight miles per hour!

It is also interesting to note that in 1968 ski jump records were set or tied in five of the eight divisions.

CHAPTER EIGHT

Trick Skiing

Trick skiing or "tricking" is gymnastics on water skis. No other kind of water skiing is as healthy, body building, or weight trimming as this form of aquacalisthenics. Once you're hooked on it, watch out; for as soon as you've mastered a couple of tricks, you'll probably rather "trick" than eat or sleep!

98. Here I demonstrate a one-ski stepover. Trick skiing is actually a form of gymnastics on water skis.

TRICK SKIS:

Trick skis are shorter and wider than standard skis, but the significant difference is the lack of any stabilizing fin. Trick skis are actually designed *not to track well* so they can travel sideways (sideslides), and backward (one-eighties)—in short, in any one of 360 degrees. They must be lightweight, short, strong, and wide enough to carry a certain amount of weight. Ski design and binder placement are very important because in trick skiing, more than in any other water skiing event, equipment plays a major role.

Years ago trick skis were just short standard skis with no fins. It was hard to turn or sideslide these models. Eventually they were widened up to eight inches (then an AWSA prescribed maximum width) which improved their maneuverability, but their straight sides hindered smooth spinning (tracking too much), and only the front tips were turned up.

Then along came the "banana peel" design, a torpedo shape around fifty-four inches long with the ski bent in a barrel-stave arc, though it was swept up more in the front. This ski performed well for trick skiers from about 1955 to the early 1960s when I became interested in trick skiing. I noticed that some competitive trick skiers had sawed off the ends of their "banana peels" and seemed to be "tricking" better. After hacking up many trick skis, I discovered how much I could improve existing designs with a saw, a plane, and some sandpaper—in about an hour's time. And each time I'd learn something. I concluded that no existing blanks then coming out of manufacturer's presses were anywhere near perfect.

I learned, for instance, that a slight dihedral angle precisely sanded, or molded into the bottom of the ski, extending to the edges, makes a very slippery trick ski handle steadier, and prevents it from catching an edge during sideslides, as sharp-edged flat-bottom skis do.

After several years of testing and research, I patented my new symmetrical trick ski, and used this design in making nine record runs and in winning four National Men's Trick Skiing

99. Trick skis I designed myself. Top view and side view. (Courtesy Superior Sports Specialties)

Championships and the 1968 National Senior Men's Tricks title.

My perfectly symmetrical trick ski is pictured above. A one-inch to one-eighth-inch dihedral prevents edge-catching and makes sideslides easier. Its arc of a perfect circle makes it possible for the skier to rotate maintaining a uniform vertical axis. The binders are placed so that the skier's shinbone line extended falls on the center of the ski. The ski has a thick, rigid center to prevent it from bending under stress and tapers thinner at the tips. Seventy percent of the ski's weight is thus concentrated underfoot, speeding turns and stepovers, and saving time in hard-pressure tournament competition. Beveled top edges all the way around the ski streamline it for less water resistance when turning. High-quality binders provide better foot control. My own trick skis are only forty inches long, and carry my 150 pounds easily.

The following is a table of the latest recommended trick ski lengths and widths depending on the skier's weight:

RECOMMENDED SIZES FOR TRICK SKIS

Skier's Weight	Trick Ski Dimensions	
	Width	Length
Under 100 lbs.	7¾"	40"
100–160 lbs.	9"	40"
160–225 lbs. and over	9"–9½"	44"

RECOMMENDED LEARNING ORDER OF TRICKS:

First concentrate on the basic two-ski tricks. When you have mastered No. 7 (back start on two skis), begin riding one ski and learning your first one-ski trick. I recommend that you learn the tricks in the following order:

Learning Order	One or Two Skis	The Trick	AWSA Symbol
1	2	Sideslide	SS
2	2	Front-to-back 180	B
3	2	Back-to-front 180	F
4	2	360 (and reverse 360)	O
5	2	Wake 180 front to back	WB
6	2	Wake 180 back to front	WF
7	2	Back start	BS
8	1	Back-to-front 180	F
9	1	Front-to-back 180	B
10	1	Sideslide	SS
11	1	Toehold front to back	TB
12	1	Toehold back to front	TF
13	2	Stepover front to back or "line back"	LB
14	2	Stepover back to front or "line front"	LF
15	2	Wake 360 front to front or "helicopter"	W FF
16	1	360 (and reverse 360)	O
17	1	Wake 180 front to back	WB
18	1	Wake 180 back to front	WF
19	2	Wake stepover front to back or "wake line back"	WLB
20	2	Wake stepover back to front or "wake line front"	WLF
21	1	Wake 360 front to front or "helicopter"	W FF

Learning Order	One or Two Skis	The Trick	AWSA Symbol
22	1	Stepover front to back or "line back"	LB
23	1	Stepover back to front or "line front"	LF
24	1	Wake line back	W LB
25	1	Wake line front	W LF
26	1	Toehold sideslide	T SS

Note: In order to group related tricks together in this book, I have not always discussed the tricks in their recommended order.

Now that you've glanced at that formidable list, let's start tricking. For your first few tricks, use a seventy-five-foot line. Familiarize your driver with the "barbell course" driving procedure, and tell him to tow you at a steady speed of seventeen miles per hour. Be sure to select the correct trick skis for your weight. They'll feel very slippery, so spend ten or fifteen minutes skiing on them as if they were standard skis. Remember that it's hard to cut on these, as they have no fins, so cross the wake and turn very gently; otherwise they'll slide out from under you. In a few minutes you'll get the hang of it and soon will know how to "edge" them. Swing back and forth across the wake for a while; then jump the wake (carefully at first). It is important that you learn the skis' handling characteristics before you even try a trick.

THE VERTICAL CROUCH:

The most solid position in trick skiing is the vertical crouch. Whether skiing forward, sideways, or backward, during all tricks described in this book if you hold the vertical crouch, you're halfway there. Staying directly over your binders, just lower your whole body by bending at the knees and waist. Half-bend your arms to bring the handle in close to your body. Keep your head up, as if looking at the horizon. Your eyes will naturally tend to look down at the water, especially when you're skiing backward. This is okay, but don't ever face down toward the water; it will throw you off balance, and get you a noseful!

Janie Peckinpaugh demonstrates the vertical crouch and bounce:

100. She is low, knees bent directly over her binders.

101. In the up part of the bounce she is careful never to straighten out fully.

102. And back to the down position. The bounce is really a "down-up-down" movement.

Your body has a tendency to follow your head. If you can keep your head turning on an even keel, chances are you will stay on an even keel.

THE LOW BOUNCE:

Like dancing, figure skating, snow skiing, or gymnastics, trick skiing requires rhythm and timing. The bounce is a springy, rhythmic down-up-down motion undertaken while crouching low in the knees. Not only does the bounce coordinate your movements during a trick, but on the up part of a bounce, your skis are unweighted, permitting easy turning.

If you turn with skis not properly unweighted you'll probably catch an edge halfway through the turn (when the skis are sideways) and almost certainly go swimming.

This is why the following instructions will almost always tell you to do a trick while "bouncing upward." A good check on yourself is to make sure that when you're at the top of the bounce, you're halfway through the trick.

IN WHICH DIRECTION WILL YOU TURN:

Of course, it is advisable to learn 180s, 360s, and helicopters in both clockwise and counterclockwise directions. However, it is possible to learn wake tricks improperly and off the wrong wake. Then, when you finally begin one-ski tricks, you may have some real trouble. It all basically goes back to which foot you are better on; and you have already found that out when learning to ride one ski. This now determines your best tricking direction, and which wake to use for wake tricks.

TRICK TURNING DIRECTION RULES:

Left-foot-forward skiers should first learn all their tricks to the left (counterclockwise) and all their wake tricks, except helicopters, off the left wake.

Right-foot-forward skiers should first learn all their tricks to the right (clockwise) and do all their wake tricks, except helicopters, off the right wake.

(Since more skiers ski with their left foot forward, most tricks are described from that viewpoint. Right-foot-forward skiers will merely have to transpose directions. When clockwise tricks are shown, left-foot-forward skiers must transpose directions.)

TWO-SKI SIDESLIDE:

Success Factor: 1 to 10 tries

After you're fairly well accustomed to your new trick skis, select the best boat speed by signaling your driver either up, down, or okay. If your skis "bog," the speed is slow. A slippery or skiddish feeling means it's too fast. A variation of one-half mile per hour can make the difference, so after you've found the correct speed, signal the driver with the "okay" sign to tell him that he should hold that boat speed exactly.

Assume a low, vertical crouch position with knees bent, head up, and arms slightly bent. Never hold your arms straight when trick skiing. Start bouncing rhythmically up and down with your knees, but never bouncing up anywhere near a straight leg position. Stay directly behind the boat, in the center of the wake.

For a sideslide to the left, bounce gently upward, simultaneously releasing your left hand, and turn left.

As soon as your skis break out of their forward track, they'll slip into a sideslide, so keep them about a foot apart for stability. Since you're traveling sideways, angle your bent knees away from the boat's pull to prevent "catching an edge" as the right sides of your trick skis become the leading edges. Hold your free (left) hand out to your side for better balance.

If your skis slide out from under under you, toward the boat, you're not low enough, or your boat speed is too fast. If you catch an edge and fall toward the boat, you're not angling your knees enough to keep the skis' side edges from catching. Remember to stay low.

103, 104, 105. Being careful to angle her knees away from the boat's pull, Janie does a two-ski sideslide.

FRONT TO BACK 180 OR "BACK":

Success Factor: 3 to 10 tries

Skiing in the center of the wake, assume a low, vertical crouch position, holding the handle in fairly close to your body, with skis about a foot apart.

For a left 180, bounce gently, and lead the turn with your head held erect. At the same time release your left hand, and pull the handle in toward your right hip with your right hand. During the turn stay low, directly over your binders, holding your head up and looking at the horizon. Pull the handle in very close to the small of your back so that your left (free) hand may quickly grasp it when the turn is complete. Finally, when you are skiing backward, both hands should be holding the handle. Whenever you're in the back position, press your knuckles against the small of your back. (This is a good gimmick to help keep the handle in close, which is so important in trick skiing.)

Should you fall either backward or forward upon completing the turn, you're not low enough, or you're not holding the handle in close enough. If you clobber (fall) even before approaching the 180 position, you're not bouncing enough.

Ski backward for extended periods; you must now learn to feel comfortable skiing this way. Soon you'll be able to cross the wake backward and even jump the wake backward.

TWO-SKI BACK TO FRONT or "FRONT":

Success Factor: 2 to 6 tries

It's very simple to turn back to the front position. Skiing backward in the low, vertical crouch position, start bouncing gently. Assuming you want to do the back to front to the left, simply let go of the handle with your right hand, and lead the turn with your head. Make sure that you hold the handle in close to your body with your left hand throughout the turn. As you reach front position, grasp the handle quickly with both hands.

If you should be thrown forward before reaching the front position, you're not holding the handle in close enough. Stay low!

106, 107, 108, 109. For the two-ski front to back, Janie keeps her head up, rope in close, and knees bent.

110, 111, 112, 113. Keeping the handle in very close, Janie bounces to the front position to her right.

114, 115, 116, 117, 118, 119. Two-ski 360. Janie is careful to keep her weight low and directly over her binders.

THREE-SIXTY OR "TURNAROUND" OR FRONT TO FRONT OR "O":

Success Factor: 5 to 15 tries

Follow all the directions for the "back" and "front," but don't stop or hesitate in the back position. Stay low in a good vertical crouch. Keep the handle in close, passing it from hand to hand smoothly, without fumbling.

Start off gradually by doing the back, hesitating, then coming to the front position. Gradually cut down the hesitation time between the tricks until they become one smooth 360 maneuver.

ROPE HANDLING—IMPORTANT PRACTICE AID:

To save yourself lots of spills, you can practice on dry land. Rig a ski rope and pulley with a twenty-five- to forty-pound weight on it (depending on your weight) in your cellar, playroom, or outside on the lawn. This simulation of the boat's pull will sharpen your rope handling without nuisance falls. Spin quickly, as if

120. Beth and I watch Janie perform a dry-land helicopter on my lawn, paying particular attention to her rope handling. We used a weight of about fifteen pounds for her.

doing 360s, and pass the rope in close from hand to hand, until you're nimble and fast with your hands.

Let me give you an illustration of the effectiveness of dry-land practice. In November 1962, after winning my first National Championship, I received an invitation to the Western Hemisphere International Water Ski Championships scheduled for early December at Miami, Florida. I had not trained in two months, because Bantam Lake, in Connecticut, was beginning to freeze over. Using this simple rope and pulley device, I trained for ten days on a frozen lawn, flew to Miami for the weekend, and won the National Men's Trick Skiing Championship.

RECOMMENDED WEIGHTS FOR ROPE AND PULLEY TRAINER

Skier's Weight	Weight of Block or Counterweight
60–80 lbs.	10 lbs.
80–100 lbs.	15 lbs.
100–120 lbs.	20 lbs.
120–150 lbs.	25 lbs.
150 lbs. and over	30 lbs. and over

WAKE TRICKS IN GENERAL:

Wake tricks are performed off that portion of the wake that forms a neat, sharp, bubble-free point, or crest. Before attempting any wake tricks, ski behind your boat at your trick speed and study its wake characteristics. Then stop the boat and shorten the rope so that you'll ski off the point when tricking. The point of the wake is affected greatly by the type of boat used and the trick speed. The following table can be used as a general guide in determining rope lengths:

RECOMMENDED ROPE LENGTHS FOR WAKE TRICKS

Trick Speed, MPH	Recommended Rope Lengths*
14	25–40 ft.
15	25–40 ft.
16	30–50 ft.
17	35–55 ft.
18	40–60 ft.
19	45–65 ft.
20	50–70 ft.

* Generally, inboards require longer trick rope lengths than outboards. That is why there is a fifteen- to twenty-foot spread in the recommended rope lengths. My personal rope length behind my eighteen-foot inboard-outboard is forty feet at eighteen miles per hour (with two skis) and forty-two feet at nineteen miles per hour (with one ski). When I practice behind my seventeen-foot inboard, I add three feet to those distances.

It is an established fact that the best speeds for beginning tricks are between sixteen and nineteen miles per hour. In general, you'll probably want your one-ski trick speed to be about one mile per hour faster than your two-ski speed.

Wake tricks, to be legal according to the official competitive rules of the AWSA, require that your skis leave the wake and make the complete turn in the air. You shouldn't "slide" the trick, or any part of it. "Sliding"—illegal or unsuccessful wake tricks—are primarily caused by prejumping the wake, i.e., beginning the trick too soon. Many budding trick skiers are naturally impatient, and they usually end up swimming. *Never start any wake trick until you've reached the crest of the wake.*

WAKE FRONT TO BACK OR "WAKE BACK": (shown clockwise)

Success Factor: 5 to 20 tries

Select your proper rope length and boat speed. Assume the vertical crouch position and drift slowly toward the right wake. When you reach the crest of the wake, make a quick little hop, lifting your skis about four to six inches off the water and simultaneously turning them 180 degrees. As your right hand lets go, your left should be pulling the handle in toward the small of your back. Lead the turn with your head erect. Remember, it must be a low hop! If you jump too high, you'll probably fall.

Upon landing, quickly grasp the handle, and try to land with your skis squarely parallel, about one foot apart.

Don't be a Wakebungler! He cuts toward that wake as if he were preparing for a running high jump, pops two feet into the air, arms flailing straight out, and lands as though he'd been hit by four Green Bay Packers linemen. You don't need speed or

Wake back. Janie makes sure to:

121. Drift toward the wake.

122. Hop and turn fast off the very crest of the wake.

123. Turn quickly in the air—but not too high.

124. And land low, keeping her head up.

height or great strength—just a little technique and a low center of gravity. Concentrate on keeping your weight over your binders.

WAKE BACK TO FRONT OR "WAKE FRONT":

Success Factor: 3 to 10 tries

After you've succeeded in making a wake back and you're skiing backward outside the wake, it's time to learn the "wake front."

In backward position, ski about six to eight feet outside the wake, and in a low, vertical crouch, holding the handle in close, drift back in toward it again. After a clockwise wake back, the wake front must be made counterclockwise or to the left.

Keeping your head up, bounce briskly when you feel the wake's crest under you, leading the turn with your head erect and simultaneously letting go with your right hand. Pull your skis up toward you on the hop to make sure they clear the wake. On landing, grasp the handle with both hands. Remember to stay low.

BACK START ON TWO SKIS:

Success Factor: 3 to 8 tries

This trick is not used frequently in AWSA competition but it's

125, 126, 127, 128. Wake front.

lots of fun, and can even be done with regular standard skis. Most skiers prefer to do it with trick skis, however.

Instruct the driver to "Hit it" gradually two or three seconds after he sees your head dunk in the water. Here's the procedure:

Get in chest-deep water and assume a straight-forward starting position, with your knees folded in toward your chest. Tell the driver to idle the boat forward in gear.

When the line tightens and pulls you slowly forward at two or three miles per hour in the water, do a 180, quickly grasping the handle and holding it directly behind your thighs. Dunk your head in the water. This signals the driver to wait two or three more seconds, giving you a little more time to get set before beginning acceleration.

As the boat picks up speed, keep your body rigid, knees slightly bent. The tails of your skis will surface first. Don't lean too much against the pull, or you'll fall on your face and get a noseful. Stay low and hold your head up. Once you're skiing backward, pull the handle up and in against the small of your back and assume a low, vertical crouch.

Two-ski back start:

129. Janie assumes a regular starting position as the boat idles slowly forward.

130. She does a 180 in the water . . .

131. . . . takes a deep breath as she grasps the handle with both hands, and, holding the handle behind her knees . . .

132. . . . dunks her head in the water as a signal to the driver.

133, 134. She holds that position until planing . . .

135. . . . then brings the handle up behind her back.

STEPOVER FRONT TO BACK OR "LINE BACK": (shown counterclockwise)

Success Factor: 10 to 25 tries

A stepover looks difficult and feels clumsy at first, but all it requires is technique and the spunk to give it a try! It's all psychological. The trick is to hold the rope very low so that you don't have to step so high.

Before going out on the water to learn this one, why not try it on the rope and pulley? Put old blankets down on the ground or floor so you won't chip or scratch your ski when it hits the ground, and wear only your stepover ski during dry-land practice. Follow the directions as if you were on the water.

To begin a stepover to the left, assume a vertical crouch, but hold the rope very low. Bounce upward smartly, simultaneously swinging your right ski up over the rope and letting go with your left hand. As your stepover ski swings over the rope, push your weight off your water ski so that you can begin turning it 180 degrees. With your body unweighted, that water ski can easily make its 180.

Remember, keep your handle hand—the one on the side of your stepover leg—low, arm almost straight. This will be strenuous at first. Always keep your head and upper torso erect, facing the horizon. When the stepover ski touches the water, keep your free hand outward for balance.

Important: A smart bounce is necessary. Don't hesitate on this trick. Step the ski over the line in one quick, smooth motion. Some skiers prefer to hold the handle with both hands during this trick, using the baseball-bat grip.

136, 137, 138, 139, 140. Line back: Here I demonstrate a stepover, which can be tricky if you don't bounce, keep your head up, and hold the rope very low.

STEPOVER BACK TO FRONT OR "LINE FRONT":

Success Factor: 5 to 15 tries

After having done a stepover front to back, ride backward keeping your head up. Hold the handle very low with one hand and stretch the other out to your side for balance.

Bounce smartly, pushing down at the water with your left ski and simultaneously bending your right knee, thereby lifting the stepover ski up over the rope. When that ski swings over the rope, turn your head to look toward the boat.

When you are in maximum "unweighted" position (in other words, when you reach the top part of the bounce), turn the water ski quickly to the front position.

The Secrets Are: 1. Hold the rope low, keeping your back arched and your head up; 2. Bounce vigorously, and 3. Keep your upper torso's weight revolving on a vertical axis over the ski.

141, 142, 143, 144, 145. Line front: A healthy bounce is necessary on this trick.

WAKE STEPOVER FRONT TO BACK OR "WAKE LINE BACK":

Success Factor: 8 to 25 tries

Begin by doing regular "water stepovers" directly across the wake. At this stage don't worry about lifting both skis off the wake. Drift toward the wake holding the rope very low. Upon reaching the crest, simply do a regular stepover. It will seem a bit harder because of the bump forming the wake, but once you master doing it this way there is only one more ingredient to add for a proper stepover: More bounce on the crest of the wake! In other words, as your water ski mounts the crest, *bounce* and push down against the wake with the water ski. That force alone will lift you six to eight inches into the air, which is high enough. From then on it's just a matter of practice to improve your form and your landings.

146, 147, 148, 149, 150, 151. Wayne Grimditch demonstrates a lively
wake line back . . .

WAKE STEPOVER BACK TO FRONT OR "WAKE LINE FRONT":

Success Factor: 5 to 20 tries

Skiing in stepover back position, about eight feet outside the wake, head up, one hand stretched out for balance, the other holding the handle very low—drift toward the wake.

When you feel the wake's crest under your skis, briskly do a regular back-to-front stepover. After doing ten or fifteen regular stepovers across the wake, begin bouncing and pushing down with more force against the water ski as it mounts the crest, thus lifting yourself into the air. You'll probably succeed in making wake stepovers easily, but polishing up your form will take some practice.

152, 153, 154, 155, 156. . . . which is followed naturally by a wake line front.

WAKE 360s OR "HELICOPTERS":

Always learn helicopters from the outside in—that is, approach the wake from the outside, and pop your helicopter off the wake, landing in the center directly behind the boat. This affords you a better landing, since it rules out side-pulls

Left-foot-forward skiers (those turning left or counterclockwise) who have been learning their wake 180s off the left wake should first try this trick off the right wake *from the outside in.*

Right-foot-forward skiers should begin practicing their helicopters off the left wake *from the outside in.*

Although helicopters are done "hand to hand" (passing the handle from one hand to the other while spinning), the easiest way to learn is to "wrap" for it.

"WRAPPING" FOR THE HELICOPTER:

To "wrap" for a counterclockwise helicopter, hold the handle vertically in a baseball-bat grip. Pull in briskly, letting go with your left hand as the handle nears your body. Keep pulling the handle in, past your right side. With your left hand, reach around your

157, 158, 159, 160. "Wrapping" for the helicopter: Wrap your arm, not the rope, across your back.

back and grasp the handle. "Wrap" your arm, not the rope, across your back. Then rest your right hand on the rope. "Wrapping" is a good thing to practice on your rope and pulley.

THE COUNTERCLOCKWISE (LEFT) HELICOPTER:

Success Factor: 5 to 30 tries

It is easier, at first, to wrap while you're inside the wake. Then, in "wrapped" position, drift about eight feet outside the right wake. Drift toward the wake in a low, vertical crouch. When you reach the exact crest of the wake, bounce straight up, leading the counterclockwise turn with your head. Try to spin on a vertical axis, head erect. During the spin your "wrapped" arm should keep tension on the rope by holding the handle in close. Try to land with

161, 162, 163, 164, 165, 166. The helicopter: Make sure to spin on a vertical axis and to keep tension on the rope with your "wrapped" arm during the spin.

bent knees, skis about one foot apart, and grasp the handle quickly with both hands.

Most skiers who are troubled by helicopters do three things wrong: 1. They prejump the wake; 2. They spin off their vertical axis, clobbering to one side or the other, and 3. They sit backward as they land. Always start the trick on the crest of the wake. When beginning the spin, pretend to tap an imaginary cloud directly above you with the top of your head to help you maintain a vertical axis spin. If you throw (or lean) your head to either side during the spin, you'll fall. Sitting or falling backward is caused by slack rope forming during the spin. This in turn is caused by improper wrapping, failure to keep tension on the rope, or cutting too hard at the wake.

If you're planning on entering competition, a hand-to-hand helicopter saves lots of wrapping time. Once you've mastered the "wrapped" helicopter, you can learn the hand to hand in twenty tries or so. Passing the handle is the tricky part. Just remember to jump higher, spin faster, and yank in the handle as you jump and spin.

As with stepovers, you'll be much better off perfecting dry-land helicopters on your rope and pulley before practicing them on the water.

INTRODUCTION TO RAMP TRICKS:

Ramp tricks are lots of fun, and, believe it or not, very easy. Most ramp tricks are done over a five-foot ramp. At first you may want to lower it to four feet, but a five-foot ramp isn't really very awesome.

One word of caution about your skis, however: If they are constructed of soft wood, or unreinforced mahogany, they'll very likely break after one or two landings, since most manufacturers don't intend their trick skis to be used on a ramp. Laminated trick skis reinforced with melamine are best for ramp tricks since their smooth surfaces provide a constant coefficient of friction on any ramp, and they don't break easily.

Skiers who like to turn clockwise or do wake tricks off the

DRIVING FOR RAMP TRICKS

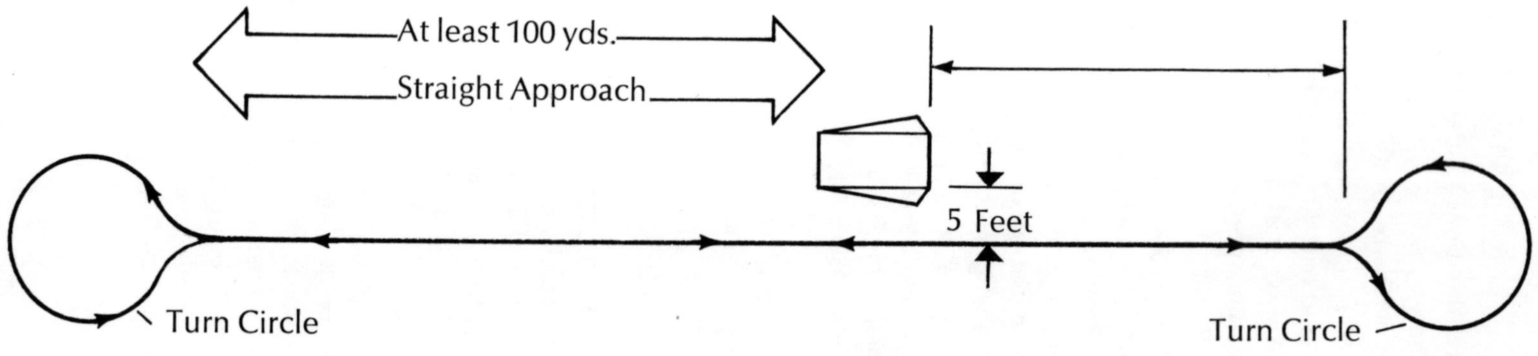

At least 100 yds.

Straight Approach

5 Feet

Turn Circle

Turn Circle

167, 168, 169, 170, 171, 172. Ramp 360: I stay low and pass the handle very low behind my thighs as soon as I touch the ramp.

right wake should have the boat pass on the left side of the ramp. Skiers who turn counterclockwise and do wake tricks off the left wake should have the boat pass to the right.

Always have the boat driven five feet from and parallel to the edge of the ramp's surface, not the sloping, protective sides (see Diagram O). That way you'll land just outside the wake.

At your usual tricking speed, make a few passes and just ride straight over the ramp until you can land without spilling or "fanny dunking." The ramp will feel very slippery, and trick skis just won't track up a waxed ramp, so assume a low, vertical crouch and make sure you're in good balance when approaching the ramp.

Before attemping tricks on the ramp, practice some very low, fast 360s and 180s on the water. Remember, on the ramp you'll be skiing uphill. Even at sixteen miles per hour, you're on the twenty-two-foot ramp surface in less than a second!

RAMP 360 OR "RAMP FRONT TO FRONT":

Success Factor: 1 to 10 tries

At ordinary trick speed or slower, approach the ramp aiming for the center in a very low vertical crouch. As your skis touch the ramp, begin a brisk turnaround, passing the handle just below your buttocks. Keep your weight evenly distributed on each ski and your head up. If you haven't finished your complete 360 by the time you leave the lip of the ramp, don't worry about it. You'll simply finish it in the air.

Rope handling is most important on this trick. Don't pop or bounce as you leave the ramp. Simply ride over the lip, not trying to get any kind of distance or height. "Giving" in the knees as you leave the ramp keeps your height and distance down, and helps improve the execution of any ramp trick sequence.

AIR 360 OFF THE RAMP OR "AIR FRONT TO FRONT":

Success Factor: 5 to 20 tries

Ride up the ramp in low front vertical crouch position, but don't start your 360 until you leave the high lip of the ramp, and don't

173, 174, 175, 176, 177, 178. Air 360: I make sure to stay low, to pass the handle quickly, and, above all, *not* to pop off the ramp.

pop or bounce. Actually, this is a helicopter off the ramp. If you do the trick "wrapped," begin spinning on a vertical axis as you leave the ramp, and treat it as you would an ordinary helicopter. If you choose to do the trick hand to hand, simply do a fast 360 in the air, making sure you quickly pass the handle in very close to your body.

RAMP 180s:

Success Factor: 1 to 10 tries

Actually, the 180 front to back on the ramp is easier than a 360, but in order to be legal in competition, the complete turn must be done on the ramp. If you're very fast, you might be able to add a 180 back to front in the reverse direction, but for the second 180 to receive credit in a tournament, it must be completed before leaving the ramp.

Most skiers are not that quick, however, and use a ramp 180 in conjunction with other tricks to make an interesting ramp sequence. The easiest to learn is the ramp back, air front combination. Simply do a front to back on the ramp, making sure you're in the back position before reaching the top of the ramp. As soon as you become airborne (not before), do an air front. The simplest way is to "tick-tock" the 180s (that is, do the ramp back to the left and the air front to the right). This way there is a definite hesitation between tricks, because of the reversal of direction. Besides, in competition, the judges can distinguish the tricks easier, which could get you more credit.

179, 180, 181, 182. Ramp 180, front to back: Staying low, I am careful to reach the "back" position at the top of the ramp.

183, 184, 185, 186. Air 180 back to front: This trick naturally follows the ramp back.

THE BACK APPROACH:

Success Factor: 1 to 10 tries

This is easy, but simply because you're approaching the ramp backward, there seems to be a psychological barrier. After the first one, you've got it made.

Ski outside the wake, heading for the center of the ramp. About thirty feet before the ramp do a low front to back. The moment your skis touch the ramp, begin a quick back to front. You'll probably finish the ramp back to front well before reaching the top of the ramp, so just continue skiing up and off the ramp.

Delaying the water front to back until you're thirty feet from the ramp is really the psychological secret. Many first-time trick skiers get in back position several hundred feet down the lake, but as they draw nearer the ramp they chicken out by doing a back to front and skiing straight up and over.

187, 188, 189, 190, 191. Back approach-ramp front combination: This is an easy trick once you've gotten past the first try.

THE BACK LANDING:

Success Factor: 5 to 30 tries

A really impressive ramp trick is the back landing. Many trick skiers seem to think you have to ski backward up and off the ramp. It can be done that way, but a much easier way is to ski frontward straight up the ramp and immediately upon becoming airborne, turn into a neat, low, 180 (air front to back) landing backward.

The secret is to settle or "crush" very low in the knees when leaving the ramp and to turn into the back position briskly, grasping the handle quickly with both hands and landing with skis one foot apart in a low, vertical crouch.

Don't let the handle pull away. Keep it in close—near the small of your back, as you do with all wake tricks. After all, it's just like doing a wake 180—off a very high wake!

MOUNTING THE BACK TRICK-SKI BINDER:

In order to do one-ski tricks, you will have to mount a back binder on one of your trick skis. The location and angle of back binder placement is very important. First, place your trick ski on the floor and put your front foot in its binder. Without looking down at your feet, place your rear foot on the ski, as close as possible to the heel of your front foot, letting it assume a natural standing angle. A left-foot-forward skier will feel most comfortable with his rear (right) foot pointing toward the right anywhere between fifteen and forty degrees. A right-foot-forward skier will find that his rear (left) foot will point at a similar angle to the left. Draw a chalk mark on the ski completely around the rear foot.

Your rear toes should be within one-half inch and no more than two inches away from your front heel. If your skis' binders do not permit your rear foot to get that close, customize them so they do. Otherwise your weight will be concentrated too far aft on the ski. Take off any dangerous metal sidebars, screws, or other sharp hardware that your rear toes might contact when kick-

Mounting the back trick-ski binder:
192. Place your rear foot on the ski in a comfortable position.

193. Draw a line around the foot.

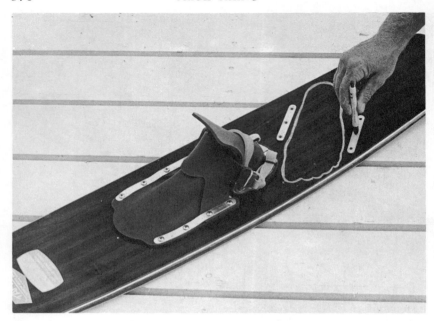

194. Position side bars on either side of the outline.

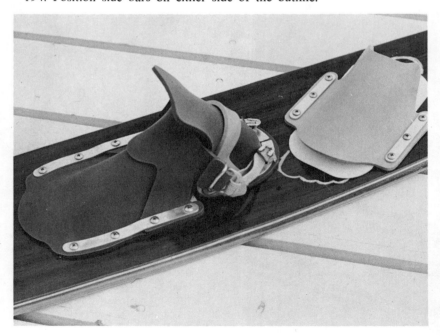

195. Mount the back binder accordingly.

ing your foot into the rear binder. To see just exactly how far your foot will go into the rear binder, first mount the binder on a plain, smooth board and try it when wet. In this way you'll find out just where to place the binder on the ski without making a mistake and possibly drilling holes in the wrong places.

After the rear binder is mounted, place some non-skid tape underfoot for better grip.

CONDITIONING FOR ONE-SKI TRICKS:

First practice riding one ski at your regular trick speed or slightly faster. Practice "slaloming" back and forth across the wake. Once the ski has slid out from under you several times, sending you swimming, you'll learn to take more care on it than on two skis. After a few practice runs, assume the vertical crouch position and jump each wake, as you "slalom" back and forth. This will train you in the rudiments of one-ski wake tricks.

196. Conditioning for one-ski tricks: Here Chris Tyll actually slaloms on one trick ski to get accustomed to it.

SKIING BACKWARD ON ONE SKI: (Preparing for the front to back)

Success Factor: 1 to 5 tries

Many skiers like to know what skiing backward on one ski feels like before they try a front to back. There are several ways to learn. One is to ski backward on two skis and pick one up in a backward salute. Simply shift all your weight to one trick ski and bend the other knee back, lifting the ski completely out of the water in salute fashion.

The other way is to ski backward on two skis, and kick one off. No matter which method you choose, don't forget to maintain a low, vertical crouch, keeping the handle in close, and your head up. Try to maintain your weight directly over your ski. As soon as you've mastered riding backward on one ski, start weaving back and forth inside the boat wakes; then carefully cross them from side to side. When you can do this successfully, you're ready for the back to front. Yes, that's right. It's easier than the front to back—so learn that first.

197. Janie demonstrates how you should learn to ride backward on one ski—by doing a backward salute.

198, 199, 200. Kicking off one ski backward: An easy way to ride one ski backward is to start on two and kick one off.

ONE-SKI BACK TO FRONT OR "FRONT":

Success Factor: 1 to 7 tries

Riding backward inside the wake on one ski in the vertical crouch position, start bouncing gently, keeping your head up. For a 180 to the right, let go with your left hand and as you bounce up, turn your head right as if intending to look toward the boat. Your head will lead the turn and your body will follow. Turn briskly, making sure your right hand keeps the handle in close during the turn. On reaching front position, grasp the handle again with both hands.

201, 202, 203. One-ski back to front: Janie simpy lets go with one hand and bounces to the front position.

ONE-SKI FRONT TO BACK OR "BACK":

Success Factor: 4 to 10 tries

Assume a low, vertical crouch position and start bouncing gently. Turn briskly on the "up" part of a bounce, release one hand (the left if you are doing the trick to the right; the right if you are doing the trick to the left), and lead the turn with your head. With your other hand keep the handle in close to your hip. Try to make a perfect 180, i.e., don't overturn or underturn. When in back position, grasp the handle quickly with both hands. Consistently falling backward when you get to the back position indicates that you have placed too much weight on your rear foot, or that you're not low enough. If you fall on your face when you get to the back position, you have too much weight on your front foot. Crouch lower!

204, 205, 206. One-ski front to back: Her head up, Janie keeps the rope in close and stays low.

ONE-SKI SIDESLIDE:

Success Factor: 10 to 30 tries

Use a seventy-five-foot rope for this trick to avoid boat turbulence as much as possible. First, assume a low, vertical crouch. For a sideslide to the left, bounce slightly, release your left hand, and turn to the left. The one-ski sideslide position will feel ten times as slippery as the two-ski, so stay low, tilting the ski's leading edge up slightly by adjusting it with your knees. Keep the handle halfway in toward your body so that you can let out or pull in farther for quick balance adjustments. Extending your free arm helps maintain balance.

You'll quickly discover your best one-ski trick speed (usually about one mile per hour faster than on two skis). If you fall forward, you're catching the leading edge. Angle it up more and make sure your boat speed isn't too fast.

Your ski may tend to slide out from under you. If this happens often, don't attempt a full ninety-degree sideslide right away, but try a forty-five-degree sideslide first, just to get the feel of sidesliding. Or try slowing the boat down a bit.

Generally speaking, balance is even more important for one-ski tricks than it is for two-ski tricks, and the techniques as described must be followed rigidly—and, of course, practiced diligently.

207, 208, 209. One-ski sideslide: With a slight bounce, Wayne snaps his ski into sideslide position. All this requires is practice.

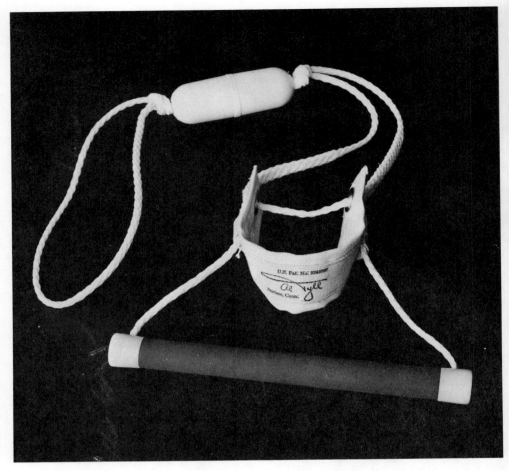

210. A trick handle. (Courtesy Al Tyll Enterprises)

THE TRICK HANDLE:

Ever since people began to do tricks on water skis, they have wanted to ski with "no hands." Some skiers have stuck their toes, heel, knee, and even their necks into the "V"-like bridle formed by the ropes connected to the handle, so that they could let go with their hands. *Never stick any part of your body through a water ski bridle unless it is specifically designed to hold it.* You can lose your finger, or hand, or toe—or neck, for that matter.

For years, trick skiers doing toehold tricks used a primitive strap fastened between the handle bridle. With the slightest jerk, or slack in the line, off came the handle! Then an elaborate trick handle was designed, using a slinglike toepiece held inside the handle bridle by a crosspiece. (Incidentally, this was also dreamed up by champion skier Stew Leonard, who invented the ski trainer.)

The trick handle toehold actually snugs up on your foot when you let go of the handle. As soon as you grasp the handle again (relieving the pull on the foot), it automatically releases. Should the skier fall, he merely has to point his toes, and the toehold sling slips off.

This toehold trick handle has really revolutionized toehold tricks, because it is comfortable, holds well, and comes off easily during a fall.

PREPARING FOR TOEHOLD TRICKS:

Practice riding in front toehold position, first inside the wake, then across the wake. Your thighs will feel shaky at first and will ache after riding in that position for a minute or two, but soon you'll begin to feel relaxed. To start shaping up for wake tricks, practice hopping off the wake three or four inches into the air each time you cross it in toehold position. Soon you'll have people in boats following you around the lake, just to watch you practice.

TOEHOLD FRONT TO BACK OR "TOE BACK":

Success Factor: 5 to 20 tries

(Left-foot-forward skiers turn left; right-foot-forward skiers, right.)

Assume the front toehold position, staying low and keeping your hands out to the side and your head up. Both "rope" knee and "water" knee should be bent. Begin bouncing slightly by bending the water knee. At the up part of a bounce, begin the 180 by turning your head in the direction you wish to go. Follow briskly with your body and ski. Try to stay low, directly above your binder, and swing your arms around as your upper torso turns. Arch your back and keep your head erect to prevent yourself from looking down at the water during the turn. Don't

211, 212, 213, 214. Toe back: With a nice bounce, Janie pivots on her ski, keeping both knees bent, head erect, and hands outstretched for balance.

straighten your knees; they must remain bent, especially the toe-hold knee.

Ride in back toehold position for a while, keeping your back arched, head up, and arms extended for balance. Skiing back and forth inside the wake this way is good toehold practice. (During a commercial picture shooting session in Florida, I twice skied two miles in back toehold position while shaving with a portable electric razor and holding a smile—but I wouldn't recommend trying anything like that before you've had a little more experience.)

TOEHOLD BACK TO FRONT OR "TOE FRONT":

Sucess Factor: 15 to 35 tries

In low "back toehold" position, knees bent, back arched, head erect, and arms extended for balance, bounce and lead the turn with your head, as if you were going to look toward the boat. As you approach the "front" position, bend forward at the waist to keep your upper torso directly over the binder. *And by all means always keep that rope knee bent.*

Most beginners fall backward upon completing the turn to front position because they don't start the turn with an arched back. Letting your rope knee pull out too straight also causes this. Try to do this trick briskly to prevent catching an edge when halfway through the turn.

215, 216, 217, 218. Toe front: Janie bounces to the front position and as she comes around, bends forward at the waist.

WAKE TOEHOLD FRONT TO BACK OR "TOE WAKE BACK":

Success Factor: 10 to 50 tries

Skiing in the center of the wake in front toehold position, crouch low and drift toward the wake, arms held out for balance.

On the crest of the wake, bounce by straightening your ski leg a little. (*Not too much. Four to eight inches will do.*) As you bounce, hold your upper torso and head over the center of the ski. Arching your back will help.

Lead the turn with your head. When the ski lifts off the wake, turn it briskly. Try to land with your ski in an exact 180 position. Your back should be arched, your head up, both knees bent, and your arms out for balance. Upon landing, don't let your face or upper torso bend down toward the water. Many, many skiers do this because they don't keep their heads up and their backs arched.

219, 220, 221, 222, 223, (*following pages*). Toe wake back: The secret of this trick is to stay erect and not to prejump the wake.

WAKE TOEHOLD BACK TO FRONT OR "TOE WAKE FRONT":

Success Factor: 20 to 70 tries

After having done the toe wake back, let yourself drift out about six feet from the wake—no farther.

In low back toehold position, with *both* knees bent, back arched, head erect, and arms extended at shoulder height for balance, drift toward the wake.

When you feel the wake's crest directly under your binder, bounce slightly, leading the turn with your head as if you wanted to look toward the boat. Many skiers fall backward a lot when first learning this trick. This can be avoided by bending forward at the waist during the last half of the turn. Keeping your rope knee half-bent will help you stay directly over your ski and prevent you from possibly losing the trick handle. As with all wake tricks, don't jump too high. In fact, at first don't concentrate on clearing the wake at all. Just get the feel of completing the trick over the wake. Never, in any case, hop any higher than six to eight inches off the wake. You don't need to. And don't prejump the wake. Wait until you feel the crest solidly under your ski.

224, 225, 226. Toe wake front: Most people fall backward on this trick as they come around. Notice how I keep my head up and bend forward at the waist as I come around to the front position.

ONE-SKI WAKE BACK:

Success Factor: 5 to 25 tries

Assume a low, vertical crouch position while skiing in the center of the wake. Drift toward the left wake. When you reach the crest of the wake, bounce, and turn your body and ski.

In general, follow the same procedure and technique you use on two skis, but your movements must be more precise. Drift, don't cut, toward the wake. Stay low. Execute the trick off the exact crest of the wake, and keep the rope in close at all times. Grasp the handle quickly with both hands again, when in the back position. Don't underturn or overturn. Try to make your turn in the air *exactly* 180 degrees. If, upon landing, you find yourself falling, crouch lower and concentrate your weight directly over your binders.

227, 228, 229, 230. One-ski wake back: Wayne is careful not to pre-jump this trick; he lands in a low crouch, handle in close.

ONE-SKI WAKE FRONT:

Success Factor: 3 to 15 tries

In backward skiing position, six to eight feet outside the left wake, begin a drift toward the wake. You should be in a low, vertical crouch, and you should hold the handle in close, knuckles touching the small of your back. As you feel the crest of the wake under you, bounce, leading the right turn with your head, as if looking toward the boat. Simultaneously, let go with your left hand. Stay directly over your binders during the turn, and upon landing grasp the handle quickly with both hands.

Most beginners "prejump" or start the trick before they reach the wake. Don't get overanxious. If you wait until you feel the wake under you, you won't even have to bounce hard because the "bump" of the wake will lift you in the air a couple of inches.

231, 232, 233, 234, 235. One-ski wake front: Wayne holds a vertical turning axis on this trick; he gets good height off the wake without even trying.

ONE-SKI 360 OR "FRONT TO FRONT":

Success Factor: 20 to 40 tries

This trick must be done smoothly and briskly, and, as with the two-ski 360, is a matter of good balance and rope handling. At first *do it purposely with hesitation.* That is, in this order: Front to back; hesitate; back to front (in the same direction). In this way you can do it in two bounces, with a "down" between bounces during the hesitation. As your rope handling improves, do the whole trick fast in one smooth bounce, completing as much of the 360 as possible during the bounce. Practice this trick in the reverse direction as much (if not more) than in your favorite direction. Many skiers consider the reverse 360 on one ski one of the hardest tricks in the book. Simply the fact that it is a reverse seems to make the trick much more difficult.

236, 237, 238, 239, 240, 241. One-ski 360: Janie makes the trick look easy, mainly because she keeps the handle in close, and her head erect.

ONE-SKI HELICOPTER OR WAKE FRONT TO FRONT OR WAKE "0":

Success Factor: 10 to 15 tries.

Wrapping for a helicopter will surprise you the first time you try it on one ski, since you don't have the stability of two, and it will tend to "unwrap" you if you don't grab the handle behind your back on the first try. If you're good at wrapping for two-ski helicopters, you'll catch on quickly. Otherwise, the basic elements of a one-ski helicopter pertain as on two skis, with the possible exception of the landing. Again, this is where experience in wake jumping on only one ski will help. Don't cut hard toward the wake. Stay low, bounce, and spin quickly, leading the spin with your head. Try to revolve on a vertical axis. Your "wrapped" arm should keep tension on the rope to prevent slack. Try to land directly over your binders. Reread the discussion of helicopters earlier in this chapter.

ONE-SKI LINE BACK:

Success Factor: 10 to 20 tries

In one way this trick is easier than a two-ski line back; at least you don't have to swing a clumsy ski over the line. On the other hand, once the trick is completed, you have no ski there to rest your weight on. Hence the drawback cancels the advantage.

Ski directly in the center of the wake with your rear foot out of the back binder. Assume a vertical crouch and hold the rope very low.

To perform a stepover to the left, bounce smartly and swing the stepover (right) leg over the rope, letting go with your left hand, and simultaneously turning your ski 180 degrees.

When the stepover is completed, don't let your free foot dig into the water. This could get you a quick dunking! However, some part of your foot must touch the water to make the trick legal according to AWSA rules, so just let your big toe dip in the water. Keep your head up at all times, and hold the handle low. (Some skiers even let one end of the handle touch the water on this one.)

242, 243, 244, 245. One-ski line back: A good bounce really helps Wayne on this trick because during the turn, his ski is almost out of the water.

ONE-SKI LINE FRONT:

Success Factor: 5 to 15 tries

After a left line back, the line front must be to the right.

Riding backward in stepover position, hold the handle very low with your right hand and point your left out diagonally for balance. Keeping your head up, bounce smartly, pushing down against the water with your ski, and swing your stepover leg (with knee bent) over the rope.

Lead the turn with your head as if attempting to look toward the boat. At the top of your bounce, your ski will be sufficiently unweighted so that it will turn easily to the front position.

Try to end the trick with your weight concentrated over the center of the ski, and quickly grasp the handle again with both hands.

246, 247, 248, 249. One-ski line front: Same old story; staying erect and bouncing makes for a good line front.

ONE-SKI WAKE LINE BACK:

Success Factor: 25 to 100 tries

As when learning two-ski stepovers, begin by doing regular stepovers directly across the wake, not worrying about making the trick legal. Remember three additional points: 1. Drift (don't cut) toward the wake; 2. Make the turn briskly, bouncing off the crest of the wake, and 3. Concentrate on making nice, neat low landings with your ski in perfect 180 position. Also, don't forget to keep your head up and the rope low. This is one of the hardest tricks—much harder than the wake line front. Practice is the only solution.

250, 251, 252, 253. One-ski wake line back: Making sure to hold a constant vertical axis, Wayne bounces off the exact crest of the wake, keeping his head up.

ONE-SKI WAKE-WAKE LINE FRONT:

Success Factor: 15 to 50 tries

Do a wake line back and ride backward about eight feet outside the wake, keeping your head up. Hold the handle very low with one hand. Point the other out diagonally for balance. Drift toward the wake. As your ski mounts the wake, push down against it and bounce, simultaneously swinging your stepover leg over the rope. Lead the turn with your head as if looking toward the boat. As your ski leaves the wake, completely unweighted, it will easily turn to the front position. Keep the handle in close and grasp it with both hands as quickly as possible, landing with your weight concentrated over the center of the ski. You needn't try to pop too high off the wake. Just concentrate on proper timing to avoid prejumping the wake.

254, 255, 256, 257, 258. One-ski wake-wake line front

PREPARATION FOR THE TOEHOLD SIDESLIDE OR "THE ONE-FOOT ONE-SKI SIDESLIDE":

Success Factor: 1 to 10 tries

The "T SS" is as much a balance trick as it is a technique trick, and it is very hard to learn in a reasonable period of time without pre-toehold-sideslide conditioning. It is basically a one-ski sideslide with only one foot on the ski—so practice just that. You'll be surprised how tricky it is!

Skiing directly behind the boat on one trick ski and holding onto the handle with one or both hands, turn into a one-ski sideslide. When you are sidesliding in good control, slowly inch your rear foot out of its binder and try to hold the sideslide. Practice this for several sessions until you can hold the sideslide for at least five seconds. Stay low, and learn to adjust the side edges of the ski by angling your knee either toward or away from the boat.

Preparing to learn the toehold sideslide:

259. With his rear foot loose in the back binder, Wayne snaps into a sideslide.

260. Holding a sideslide position, he pulls his rear foot out of the binder.

THE TOEHOLD SIDESLIDE OR "TOE SLIDE":

Success Factor: 50 to 250 tries

Practice this trick first in very calm water, inside the wake, using a seventy-five-foot rope to avoid boat turbulence. Assume a low front toehold position, both knees bent, weight concentrated right over the binder. Begin bouncing gently. At the "up" part of a low bounce, when the ski is unweighted, *snap* it out of its forward track into sideslide position. Don't lead the turn with your head; otherwise you'll wind up doing a 180. Instead, keep your head reasonably erect, facing forward, eyes looking at the water maybe five feet ahead of you. This way your peripheral vision will keep the ski and water in sight. Extend your arms like balancing poles: one to the side, and one to the front. Quick balance and ski-angle adjustments are always necessary on this trick. If you think other sideslides feel skiddish, wait until you try this one!

For a "T SS" to be legal in competition, the ski must be held in a sideslide for at least 1½ (very long) seconds. If you intend to use a "T SS" in competition some day, better learn to do it for five or six seconds during training—to make sure you can hold it for two under pressure!

While practicing, you can save many nuisance falls by "recovering" to either front or back toehold position when you sense a fall coming. Snap into a good sideslide, no matter how short, then recover. Start by holding it a half second or even shorter—just as long as you're satisfied that the ski was sidesliding. Then increase it to three-quarters of a second; then one, and so on. If you use this method, and have a long summer ahead, you might learn a good two-second "T SS" in two or three months.

Toehold sideslide:

261. In low front toehold position . . .

262. . . . I snap my ski into a sideslide . . .

263. . . . and try to stay low, both knees bent, arms outstretched for better balance.

CHAPTER NINE

Riding the Saucer

While saucer riding is not considered true water skiing, it is an enjoyable change of pace and employs fundamentals which may be helpful in trick skiing, such as good balance and deft rope handling.

The average saucer is basically a round disc of one-half- to three-quarters-of-an-inch marine plywood twenty-four to forty-two inches in diameter. Most saucers on the market today are flat, but a small group of saucer specialists prefer saucers with convex bottoms, claiming that these track better and don't "dive" as easily.

Saucers cost anywhere from twenty to thirty dollars apiece, but there's no reason why you can't find a leftover chunk of marine plywood at a lumber yard and cut out a perfect thirty-six-inch circle. Bevel both top and bottom edges about one-eighth of an inch, and sand all surfaces well. Give the saucer at least two coats of varnish, urethane, or marine enamel. Put some non-skid tape on the top side to provide a sure footing for the rider. One manufacturer attaches toepieces on their saucers for sure footing, but this can have a drawback because most riders frequently shift position.

Since a saucer has a large planing surface (a thirty-six-inch saucer has over one thousand square inches), very little speed or power is required for it to carry even a heavy person. Outboards with as little as ten horsepower may be sufficient, but any ski towboat will do for saucer towing, whether inboard or outboard.

Naturally, the weight of the rider determines the desired speed,

264. The saucer: This saucer has toepieces, but many saucer experts feel that binders hinder them from making subtle changes in position. (Courtesy Cypress Gardens Skis, Inc.)

265. Scotty Loomis feels right at home on a saucer.

but most people like between fourteen and eighteen miles per hour. Light youngsters can go as slow as nine or ten miles per hour.

YOUR FIRST SAUCER START:

Saucers of thirty to thirty-six inches are easiest to learn on. Wade out into waist-deep water, lie down on the saucer, and hold the tow handle and leading edge just out of the water with both hands. (If you held the saucer with one hand and the towbar with the other, you'd be pulled sideways at the start.) Tell the driver to *idle* the boat forward.

As the rope tightens, pull your knees up and kneel on the saucer with your feet just off the trailing edge. Then signal the boat driver to "Hit it." He should accelerate slowly until the saucer is planing. Wait until the speed feels comfortable before you try to stand up. This requires slow, careful movements.

Let go of the towbar with one hand, say the left (although it doesn't matter which), and place that hand on the saucer in front of your left knee. Lift your left leg up and place your foot flat on the saucer just behind and to the outside of your left hand. Remember, jerky movements may throw you off balance.

Then transfer the towbar to your left hand, position your right hand in the same manner, and place your right foot on the saucer to assume a squatting stance. Make sure your feet are about eighteen inches apart and just behind the saucer's center line before you slowly rise to standing position. Don't stand too tall! Stay in a vertical crouch to keep a low center of gravity. Should you want to move your feet to a better position, slide them— don't pick them up! Lifting them off the saucer will shift your weight too radically, causing the saucer to bog or slide out from under you. If the front of the saucer tends to "dive," move your weight back a bit. If it rides too high or "porpoises," you're too far back. Generally, keep your weight in the middle of the saucer, with a gentle lean against the pull of the boat.

After falling, stay under water a few seconds and hold your hands in front of your face when surfacing. This could prevent a nasty bruise from the very hard edge of the saucer which may still be floating in your direction.

266, 267, 268, 269, 270, 271. Your first saucer start.

A planing saucer offers little drag on the boat, and seems to glide effortlessly across the water. Therefore, should you yank on the rope too hard you'll find yourself with a lot of slack; handle the rope gently.

After some practice, you'll be able to start right out in squatting position on the saucer and stand up as soon as it planes. This is a little tricky because you have to plant your feet just right.

DRIVING THE BOAT:

Never accelerate or decelerate rapidly or jerkily while towing a saucer rider. Make speed changes gradually. Backing off on the throttle too fast will cause slack rope, giving the saucer rider real problems. Making sharp turns will whip him out of control outside the wake at high speed. Stay a good distance from shore and from other boats.

STEERING THE SAUCER:

As they say, "A saucer may slip when you want it to slide," since it doesn't have any fin or stabilizing devices. One thing is for sure: You'll never be able to turn it like a slalom ski!

Nevertheless, controlling a saucer is basic. To go left, simply lean to the left; to go right, shift your weight to the right. The saucer will turn easily, but like it or not, your turns will be gradual. At first practice staying inside the wake. "Slalom" the saucer from just inside the left wake to just inside the right wake and vice versa until you can build up some steady momentum in either direction.

CROSSING THE WAKE:

This is a tricky maneuver requiring good saucer momentum or some driver cooperation and is generally easier behind a boat having a small wake.

To cross the wake on the right, first drift to just inside the left wake. Then lean to the right as hard as you dare without spilling to build up enough momentum in that direction to carry you across the wake. You should be able to master this in a few

272, 273, 274, 275. Crossing the wake: Scotty merely leans in the direction he wishes to travel, but you can't hurry the saucer. It takes its own sweet time.

tries, but if the wake keeps warding you off toward the inside, ask the driver to begin a moderate *left turn* as you are cutting toward that right wake. This will create a gentle crack-the-whip effect, and its centrifugal force will add to your saucer momentum, swinging you outside the wake. Take care to keep the leading edge of the saucer up so that it doesn't "dive" into the wake. (The "leading edge" is the edge facing the exact direction in which the *saucer* is traveling.)

As soon as you're outside the wake, the boat should straighten out; otherwise the crack-the-whip effect could double or triple your speed and possibly send you tumbling.

Once you've made it outside the wake with the boat going straight, continue to lean toward the outside; otherwise you'll drift back inside the wake.

THE SAUCER DOCK START:

Sitting on the edge of the dock, float the saucer beneath your feet, and plant them about eighteen inches apart and just behind the center line (or where you usually stand while riding the saucer). The leading edge of the saucer will thus be held about two or three inches out of the water.

Tell the driver to begin slow acceleration when the rope tightens. Take no slack rope or you'll be snapped off the dock too fast. At the moment of takeoff, crouch low on the saucer, with your arms half-bent.

Saucer dock start:
276. Sitting on the dock, Scotty presses the saucer in the water and places his feet just behind the center line.

277. As the boat pulls him off the dock . . .

278. . . . the leading edge of the saucer surfaces, but Scotty still crouches low for a surer stance.

279. He relaxes somewhat as he rides away.

SAUCER TURNAROUNDS:

There are three things to remember when doing tricks on a saucer: 1. Stand in the center of the saucer in a low, vertical crouch; 2. Keep the rope in close to your body for ease in passing the handle from hand to hand, and 3. Transfer your weight from your heels to your toes when doing a front to back; otherwise you may be pulled over backward, causing the leading edge of the saucer to dive. When turning from back to front, shift your weight from your toes to your heels again.

Rope handling is much the same as in trick skiing, but not at all as critical. As you turn, pass the handle smoothly from one hand to the other, keeping it in close to your body. One young fellow at Wild Goose Camp for Boys in Harmony, Maine, did 156 consecutive 360s!

From here on, you're on your own! The saucer can be used in

a variety of ways. Many enthusiasts do gymnastics on saucers, such as handstands and headstands. Some ride on chairs, tables, stepladders, barstools, and other contraptions placed on saucers. Members of the Laurel Water Ski Club of Highland Lake, Connecticut, constructed a huge saucer six feet in diameter. Six riding this saucer at once have a hilarious time! Earl Iffland, one of that club's fine saucer daredevils, purposely instructs the boat driver to whip him around a sharp circle during ski shows and thrills the crowds at speeds of fifty to sixty miles per hour! Some people give their pets a saucer ride. Dogs particularly seem to love it. One character even gave a trained elephant a ride! As you can see, all you need is a saucer and lots of imagination.

280, 281, 282, 283. Turnaround on a saucer: With feet spread about eighteen inches apart and approximately in the center of the saucer, Scotty merely passes the handle from hand to hand.

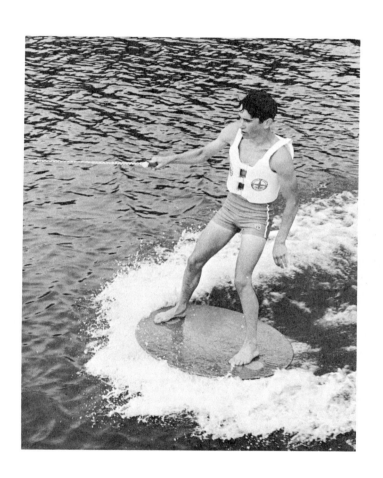

284. Joker Osborn cutting hard on shoe skis. (Courtesy Cypress Gardens)

CHAPTER TEN

Shoe Skiing

Ever feel like just plain horsing around on water skis? Try the "shoes."

Shoe skiing is an exciting challenge to the intermediate skier and is great fun at ski parties. You'll be surprised at how much can be accomplished on those midget water skis!

Most shoe skis are six to eight inches wide and fourteen to eighteen inches long. In fact, there's barely room on them for the binders. They come in rectangular, oval, or tapered shapes, usually without fins or skeds. They are not used in sanctioned competitions, except occasionally by some imaginative mixed doubles team as a dramatic finale.

WHAT SHOULD YOUR SHOE-SKI SPEED BE?:

Using standard shoe skis, the following is a good rule:

RECOMMENDED SHOE-SKI SPEEDS

Skier's Weight	Boat Speed
100–150 lbs.	22–26 mph
150–200 lbs.	24–28 mph
200 lbs. and over	26–32 mph

Before starting off, tell the driver at what speed you wish him to level off.

285. Shoe skis with starter ski.

GETTING UP ON SHOE SKIS:

There are several ways to get up on shoe skis. By far the easiest is to start out on a saucer. Once the saucer is planing, extend both shoe skis off the saucer's leading edge, making sure to keep their tips up. Then signal the driver to accelerate to proper speed, and merely stand up on the shoe skis. The saucer will float away behind you.

The next easiest way is off a dock using a special starter ski which is available with most shoe-ski sets at extra cost. Instead of having a binder, this starter ski is recessed to hold one shoe ski in place. With both shoe skis on your feet, simply place the one on your slalom foot (the foot on which you usually put your slalom ski) on the starter ski, and start out from the dock as you normally would. But don't drag your free shoe ski in the water;

Stepping off the starter ski:

286. Having started with a starter ski, Pete Knapp merely steps off it . . .

287. . . . and shoe skis away.

Deep-water shoe-ski start:

288. Pete pulls his knees in close to his chest . . .

289. . . . and holds that position as the boat accelerates.

290. His shoe skis begin to plane as the boat gains speed.

291. When it reaches twenty-two to twenty-six miles per hour, he can relax.

keep it tip up in regular starting position. Stay in the center of the wake. When the proper boat speed is reached, lean at least half your weight onto your free shoe ski, and quickly but smoothly slip your other shoe ski from the starter ski, placing it on the water *tail first*. This starter ski can also be used for easy deep-water starts.

Another common shoe-ski start is from the water while straddling a standard ski. In water waist deep (or deeper), clamp one standard ski between your thighs. Grasping the towbar with both hands, assume the normal vertical crouch starting position, knees bent, pointing your shoe-ski tips upward. Your skis will naturally be under water until the boat picks up speed. Brace yourself rigidly in the starting position until you are planing. When the proper speed is reached, stand up carefully. The standard ski will be left floating on the water.

The toughest (but most rewarding) way to start out on shoe skis is the deep water shoe-ski start, *without a starter ski or saucer*. You'll think your arms are about to be yanked from their sockets, and you'll surely get a noseful of water, but once you practice and master this start it will seem progressively easier. Simply get in water waist deep (or deeper), pull your knees in close to your chest (almost cannonball position) and, holding your shoe skis very close together, tell the driver, "Hit it hard!" The faster his acceleration, the quicker you'll plane. Use the solid baseball-bat grip on the handle; otherwise it may be pulled from your grasp. This is tough. Don't try it unless you're in good physical condition, or a pulled muscle or wrenched back may result.

SKIING ON SHOE SKIS:

Shoe skiing is best accomplished in calm water. Rough water can cause the tips to dive if you're not careful.

Stay directly behind the boat. Your shoe skis will wobble at first; this is because you're naturally tense and keep overreacting. It's hard to think about relaxing, since there is always a strain on your legs and knees while shoe skiing, but you must try to relax a little. Keep your shoe skis a foot or more apart, and stay in a low,

292, 293, 294. Jumping off the saucer with shoe skis is an exciting and easy trick. Just be sure you keep the tips of your shoe skis up, as Pete Knapp is doing.

vertical crouch with a slight backward lean (to keep your tips up). Remember: One false move may spill you, and shoe-ski spills, usually very sudden and without warning as tips catch, etc., can really slam you into the water. The best way to fall is to sit backward, but since most spills are edge-catching, triplike falls, it is usually all you can do to roll forward with head and body tucked.

Don't dawdle when crossing the wake. Cross it at a rather sharp angle *keeping those tips up!*

Pick the speed that is most comfortable—that is, at which your shoe skis plane easily and the spray is least bothersome.

TRICKS ON SHOE SKIS:

After Eastern Over-All Champion Stew Leonard had set a new world trick skiing record at the Lake Lashaway Open, in East Brookfield, Massachusetts, in 1959, he astounded the crowd by doing most of this trick run on shoe skis. He wetted down the ten-foot-wide starting dock and started by skiing off that onto the water's surface. He then proceeded to do 180s, 360s, wake 180s, helicopters, stepovers, and back swans.

A few years later, in 1962, while we were skiing together on Bantam Lake, Leonard challenged me to a "duel" on shoe skis. First Leonard went out and did all the aforementioned tricks, plus a toehold front to back. However, he fell on the toehold back to front. "Beat that!" he said, laughing, and shoved me into the water with his shoe skis.

Though I was National Trick Skiing Champion, my shoe-skiing experience was limited. It took me four tries to make the deep-water shoe-ski start. Nevertheless, I made every trick Leonard had plus a half dozen toehold front to backs and back to fronts. Leonard sat in the boat shaking his head. To really rub it in, I then wrapped for a toehold wake 360, but fell in the attempt.

Generally speaking, tricks on shoe skis are similar to those in trick skiing, but more care and a lower body stance is necessary. On wake tricks don't jump high. Just hippity-hop at the crest. A most spectacular trick is the back swan. If you usually shoe ski between twenty-two and twenty-six miles per hour, do this at the high speed (twenty-six miles per hour). First do a front to back. Carefully shift your weight to your slalom-ski foot and lean away from the boat until the boat's pull and your lean are equalized. Then slowly pick up the other shoe ski. Bending that knee back toward your head and arching your back gives the trick a swanlike grace.

295. Pete does a back swan on shoe skis.

CHAPTER ELEVEN

Barefoot

Try to find a prouder boy or girl than one who has just learned to barefoot. I doubt if you can. There's something almost magical about skimming over the water on nothing but your bare feet. No matter how many times you've seen it or done it, the satisfaction and thrill is always apparent. Besides, the moment you become a "barefooter" you somehow join a higher echelon of skiers.

A FAST, POWERFUL BOAT:

Learn barefoot behind a boat that can pull a slalom skier at thirty-six miles per hour or faster. If you have average feet for your weight and size, thirty-four miles per hour should be your barefoot speed. If, however, you have smaller feet than normal, thirty-six miles per hour is recommended. Of course, a competent boat driver and observer are essential.

SEVERAL WAYS TO LEARN BAREFOOT:

Always wear a ski vest, jump jacket, or other good flotation while barefooting. Rough-and-tumble forward spills should be expected. The best way to fall, of course, is to sit backward, but this is generally not possible. The moment you feel yourself falling forward, try to tuck into a ball, and by all means *close your eyes;* water splashing into them at thirty-six miles per hour really stings. Always use a seventy-five-foot standard rope length, and at least for learning, pick a long, calm stretch of water.

A good method of preparing for barefoot is to ride a slalom ski and practice "digging in" your free foot heel first as hard as you can without flipping. If your slalom ski begins to feel "spongy" you're getting somewhere, because that means some of your weight is being borne by the bare foot.

THE STEPOFF METHOD:

This is the most common barefoot start; you use a standard ski as a "starter" or freeboard, much as in shoe skiing. The best kind of starter ski is one with the binder removed and non-skid material pasted where the binder was. Getting up on this starter ski is a bit trickier than getting up on a slalom ski because of the lack of a binder, but as soon as the boat idles forward, the water pressure against the ski will keep it in place against your foot.

The best place to step off is five to ten feet outside the wake. Left-footed skiers should step off outside the left wake; right-footed skiers, outside the right wake.

Instruct the driver to give you a normal deep-water slalom ski takeoff start but to accelerate temporarily to only twenty-two miles per hour. This gives you time to ski carefully outside the proper wake. When you're out there, assume a "sitting-in-a-chair" position and signal the driver to accelerate to your recommended barefoot speed. Don't step off until he or the observer signals that barefoot speed has been reached.

Press your free foot into the water heel first about eighteen inches from the freeboard and slightly forward of the other foot. Your arms should be slightly bent. Don't hesitate to lean back hard agains the boat's pull during the stepoff.

When your bare foot feels as though it's carrying more than 50 percent of your weight, briskly slip the other foot off the freeboard, preferably to the outside, and dig it, heel first, into the water.

THE CRUCIAL MOMENT AFTER STEPOFF:

Most spills are caused by an improper stepoff. Keep your toes curled up or else you'll "catch a toe," which is just like catching a tip with shoe skis. Remain crouched low as if sitting in a chair.

The stepoff method:

296. Pete Knapp skis far outside the left wake on a slalom ski . . .

297. . . . and digs his free foot into the water.

298. Then he steps out of the slalom ski . . .

299. . . . and digs his other heel into the water. Notice the low "sitting" position.

In three or four seconds you'll be barefooting. You may then straighten your arms and back a bit, but don't get too frisky right away—stay low!

After a few barefoot runs, you'll no doubt succeed in stepping off every time. At this point you can begin crossing the wake. Stay low, and remember to keep your toes curled up. Should you encounter rough water, lean back lower.

HOW TO END YOUR BAREFOOT RUN:

This is the simplest part. Merely let go of the handle, and sit backward. It will feel as though you're going down a water slide, but in ten or twenty feet you'll sink into the water. World champion Jimmy (the Flea) Jackson always did a spectacular front flip ending right in front of the crowd at tournaments and exhibitions. He would throw the handle up in the air, then swing both hands downward and tuck his body. At the same time his heels would dig into the water, flipping him through a perfect front somersault.

THE SAUCER START:

Just as easy as the stepoff method is the saucer start, which is very similar to the saucer shoe-ski start. Use a one-hundred-foot rope to get farther from the boat's turbulence, and stay *inside* the wake. When the saucer is planing, extend both feet off its leading edge and signal the driver to accelerate quickly to barefoot speed. Then dig in your heels and stand up to the "sitting" position. Many experts think this is the easiest barefoot starting technique.

SHOWY BAREFOOT STARTS:

The "jump-out" is really spectacular. Skiing outside the wake at barefoot speed, the skier leaps out of his skis, assuming a "sitting" position in the air. Leaning slightly backward, he brings his heels down in front of him. As his full weight descends, he may actually "fanny-dunk," but if he hangs on through this crucial moment, he won't penetrate the surface and will end up barefooting away.

The jump-out: Using a one-hundred-foot rope and skiing inside the wake at thirty-seven miles per hour, Pete Knapp:

300. Jumps out of both skis . . .

301. . . . assumes a "sitting" position in the air . . .

302. . . . and as his heels touch, straightens his legs . . .

303. . . . and barefoots away.

The formidable deep-water barefoot start shouldn't be tried unless you're rugged and strong. Many skiers do this trick in a literally backbreaking manner—with their legs and feet pointing toward the boat and bodies bent sharply forward at the waist, as if they were trying to touch their toes with the toebar. Well, evidently it works for them. However, jumping champion Penny Baker, who starred in the 1964–65 New York World's Fair water ski show and did this trick four times a day, seven days a week, described his method as being much easier. Since the pull is so severe, he sinks into the water, points his feet toward the boat, grips the handle tightly, and "locks" it by pressing it against his thighs. As the boat accelerates, he *actually arches his back,* forming a flat "ski" with his body. This way he surfaces quicker and begins riding along on his thighs. At thirty-two miles per hour or better, he drops his heels into the water and stands up. Makes a lot of sense, doesn't it?

Deep-water barefoot start:

304. Pete waits until the line tightens as the boat idles away.

305. He then sinks into the water, pointing his feet toward the boat.

306. As the boat accelerates, he hangs on for dear life and planes on his thighs and back.

307. Nearing proper barefoot speed, he digs in his heels . . .

308. . . . "relaxes" into "sitting" position and rides away.

BAREFOOTING OFF THE BEACH:

Put on two old bathing suits and select a gradually sloping sandy beach, free of rocks, broken glass, etc. Holding the towbar, position yourself about fifty feet from the water's edge.

As the boat accelerates, run toward the water, keeping the line taut. About five feet from the water's edge, throw both feet out in front of you and slide on your fanny (that's why the two suits!) into the water. Keep your feet high so they won't dig into the sand or water.

If you do this correctly, you won't sink into the water but will ride along on your thighs and legs. Hold your feet just out of the water, toes pointing toward the boat and simply hang on, pressing the handle against your thighs. At twenty-five to thirty miles per hour simultaneously ease both heels into the water. Above thirty-two miles per hour you can rise and barefoot away.

The secret of this trick is for the boat to be traveling at least twenty mph as you sit down at the water's edge. This will keep you planing. Also, be careful to ease both heels into the water at the same time. Otherwise you may be pulled off balance to one side.

Beach barefoot:

309. Wearing a tough old pair of pants, Pete stations himself about fifty feet from the water's edge.

310. When the rope tightens, he runs a few steps . . .

311. . . . then sits down in the sand, with his feet out in front.

312. He is dragged at increasing speed to the water's edge . . .

313. . . . but the boat speed is still not fast enough for barefooting, so he planes over the water on his legs and thighs until proper barefoot speed is reached.

314. Finally, he digs in his heels and stands up.

ONE-FOOT BAREFOOT:

Many people think this is impossible, but it is really not much harder than on two feet. Add two to four miles per hour to your normal barefoot speed, and attempt this only outside the wake where the solid, smooth water is—not in the boat's residual turbulence. Slowly shift your weight to your slalom foot, lean back, and gently lift the other. The spray will be increased, of course, but that just makes the trick more spectacular. Be careful when you put the other foot back down on the water again. Gently, gently is the trick.

315. Pete demonstrates one-foot barefoot. He requires a speed of forty miles per hour, and must do it outside the wake, to achieve more solid water.

316. A mixed doubles routine is always a favorite at ski shows. (Courtesy Cypress Gardens)

CHAPTER TWELVE

Mixed Doubles

From a casual date on skis to an intensely competitive team event, mixed doubles in its various forms covers a tremendous range of possibilities. When well executed, a mixed doubles routine is one of the most beautiful and spectacular forms of skiing, with great variety between different team performances. Any mixed doubles routine is essentially a ski show executed by a boy and a girl on skis. Whether it is done purely for the joy of skiing together or as part of a carefully planned and timed routine for national competition, this type of skiing inherently involves showmanship and variety. In tournament skiing, a time limit and general rules outlining the event serve as the only restrictions to the imagination in planning and developing a performance.

The many possibilities for double skiing can be loosely grouped as "lifts and carries," "side-by-side skiing," and "specialty skiing," such as jumping or shoe skiing. Most people associate double skiing only with lifts and carries, but the other categories increase the fun and really are a necessary part of any good ski show or competitive routine. Since there are so many variations possible, there is no special requirement that a team must consist of a "superman teamed with a ballerina." Skiing doubles can be fun for almost any combination if a little careful thought is put into the equipment and the skiing routine.

EQUIPMENT:

The type of equipment you can use ranges from the very simple to the complex and expensive, depending on your interest, proficiency, and type of routine. However, most basic doubles skiing can be done with simple equipment.

The towboat can be powered by an engine with as little as forty horsepower, but really satisfying skiing requires something on the order of seventy-five horsepower, particularly if the team is heavy. It is especially important that the boat maintain pull while making a turn, and to be sure it does boat trimming may be necessary. The ski line attachment must be at the same point for both lines. It should be strong enough to withstand pulls of eight hundred pounds, and it should be placed properly close to the center of the transom or near the center turning axis of the boat so that the extra load will not affect the boat's handling characteristics. Speeds usually range from eighteen to twenty-eight miles per hour, although double barefoot acts require thirty-four miles per hour.

The skis chosen for climbing maneuvers should be sturdy and should have a fairly large surface area. Jumping skis are ideal, but a stout pair of regular skis will do fine. Many side-by-side tricks can be done with both partners on similar skis, but further variations can be attained by using trick skis or other special skis.

Both towlines should usually be the same length, but in some cases the climbing partner's line might be up to six or eight inches longer. The longer line is helpful if the boy is very tall.

As you progress into show or competitive skiing, you will want to add other refinements, such as costumes and special ski binders.

BEFORE YOU SKI—BOAT DRIVING, PLANNING, DRY-LAND PRACTICE:

In any form of doubles skiing, the boat driving is critical to the performance. And the driving is more complicated than for most other forms of skiing. In addition to the problems of speed control and maneuvering, the doubles driver must take great care to: 1. Keep his team planing at proper speed throughout all turns; 2. Vary his speed and path to suit the routine, and 3. Control the start and finish of the routine. An alert observer is, of course, vital to the process. Insofar as possible, it is best to drive the basic "barbell" pattern, but this may be varied if tricks are to be performed during the turns or if the jumping ramp is to be used.

Each run should be planned before you proceed out onto the water. This allows the boat driver to have an idea of the maneuvering pattern and will save a lot of hesitation in what may be awkward positions. When you are planning a routine, whether it be for fun or competition, keep in mind the abilities of the skiers, the water conditions, and the audience, if there is one. There are so many variations possible that it can be a lot of fun to think up the best routine for any given team.

If you have tried trick skiing, you are probably familiar with the advantages of practicing your maneuvers on shore with a practice line. This technique is extremely useful in learning mixed doubles—especially the climbing tricks. Pick a nice, soft lawn area to cushion any possible falls, and rig two lines of the same length. Almost all the climbing tricks can be practiced in this manner, and it is more convenient and quicker to work out the maneuver here than behind the boat. If you seem to have a problem, take heart; climbs are usually much easier on the water than they are on land. Getting wet before practicing is often helpful so that you will be able to slide into position easier.

CLIMBING TRICKS:

The various carries and lifts are limited only by the relative size of the partners, their physical capabilities, and their imagination. The team gets started with some method of climbing or mounting and then begins a routine involving a series of positions or poses that flow well together. It is usually easier to have the climbing pattern mount to a relatively "high" position and work down, rather than to try to start at ski level and climb gradually up.

The key to carry maneuvers is not brute strength but rather weight distribution, balance, and timing. The team should plan to be in a comfortable and stable position during the turns and to do most of the maneuvering on the straightaways. Difficult or awkward positions should be performed quickly to avoid tiring the skier doing the carrying.

CLIMBING OR MOUNTING:

The climb or mount can best be done by the conventional "stirrup climb," the "skater's flip," or by starting on the same pair of skis.

The "stirrup climb" is the easiest method. It begins by having the partners ski side by side at about twenty miles per hour. The boy bends slightly and cups his hand to form a "stirrup." The rider kicks off one ski (whichever she prefers) and puts her free foot in his hand. At the count of three she kicks off her other ski and swings that leg over his shoulder to assume a shoulder-sitting position or "topside tandem." By straightening slightly and lifting the "stirrup," the mount is made easier, but too much spring can result in the rider going off on the other side.

The "skater's flip" is more spectacular, and will require a little more practice. This begins with the boy placing his inside arm across the front of the girl's stomach and around her back. The girl kicks off one ski (whichever she prefers). Then at the count of three she kicks her feet forward, up, and out of the remaining ski, tucking to make the flip easier. Simultaneously she releases her own handle.

The boy flips the girl up to his shoulder, leaning slightly away to counteract the weight shift. It is important for the girl to go from a tuck to a straightened position at the end to make a clean finale. The resulting "forward layout" is very graceful, with the girl balancing on her stomach across the boy's shoulder.

Important Note:

During any climb or mount, when the girl drops her towline, the observer in the boat should immediately pull her line and handle into the boat.

Starting on the same pair of skis is basically simple, but requires a powerful towboat and a strong boy. Many starting positions are possible and have their respective advantages depending on your routine. The easiest way is to have the partners facing each other with the girl's legs wrapped around the boy's waist. The key to this start is to have the boat idle forward while the skiers are getting ready, allowing them to assume their positions more easily. Starts using a cross-arm carry, with the girl lying across the boy's arms, are more graceful but cause more drag and require more power.

The stirrup climb. Rit Forcier and Paula Geitz show how it's done:

317. The couple skis side by side.

318. Paula kicks off one ski and begins the climb.

319. She swings one leg over Rit's shoulder . . .

320. . . . then completes the climb and locks her feet around his back.

321. Finally, her rope is pulled into the boat.

LIFTS AND CARRIES:

The topside tandem is the most comfortable, the most stable, and one of the most graceful of the carries. It is well suited to wake crossing and rhythmic skiing. The appearance is enhanced if the girl keeps her arms out and sways with the turns to help balance. The boy should keep his back straight and absorb any rough water with his knees to lessen fatigue.

A spectacular position that flows from this is the "layback." The girl locks her ankles under her partner's wrists and eases herself back until she has her hair practically in the skis' rooster tail (the spray coming from the tail of the ski). For a more advanced carry she can release one leg. In order to recover, the girl straightens back to the topside tandem with the help of a push down on her ankles.

Another spectacular position which can easily be attained from the topside tandem is the "Statue of Liberty." While still sitting on the boy's shoulders, the girl places her feet high on his thighs.

322. Two-foot layback.

323. One-foot layback.

324. From the topside tandem position . . .

325. . . . Paula places her feet on Rit's thighs . . .

326. . . . and stands up, leaning forward against the handle. Remember, always smile, as Rit and Paula are doing, and try to keep your actions smooth and graceful.

327. Low forward layout.

The boy then crouches a bit to prevent the girl's feet from slipping as she stands up and leans forward to rest her thighs on his forearms, simultaneously arching her back and spreading her arms gracefully.

To regain the topside tandem position, the procedure is simply reversed; or, to get into a low forward layout position, the girl reaches down, grabbing the boy's wrists and straddles the boy's waist. Once her legs are in position, she merely lets go of his wrists and rests her stomach on the towbar, extending her arms gracefully to the sides.

To assume a standing position on the skis, she locks one arm around the boy's neck and swings her feet down to the skis.

The standing doubles is perhaps the most spectacular of all carries, but it requires excellent balance and some special equip-

Standing doubles:

328. From the topside tandem position . . .

329. . . . Paula begins to stand up on Rit's shoulders as he steadies her.

330. Then, releasing Rit's hand, she stands up and leans back on her own rope.

ment. Attached to the boy's line, about ten feet from his own tow-bar, there should be an extra piece of rope with a small handle for the girl to hold when she stands up. This extra line should be from twelve to eighteen inches longer than the boy's, depending on the girl's height. In order to keep it out of the way while performing other tricks, it can be attached to the boy's bridle with a clip or other fastening device. When the girl is ready to stand up, he can simply unhook it and hand it to her.

From the topside tandem position the girl holds her rope in one hand and the boy reaches up to hold her other hand. She then brings one foot at a time up to his shoulders, being very careful not to lurch forward or backward. From there she slowly stands up, releasing the boy's hand. The girl should lean back on her own line; this action not only looks better but is also much more stable. Reverse the procedure to regain the topside tandem position.

The forward layout on one shoulder, the position resulting from a skater's flip, can also be easily attained from a topside tandem. The girl unlocks her legs from inside the boy's arms, leans forward to hold the boy's arms, and straightens her legs. The boy releases the towbar with one hand and reaches up to brace his partner on his shoulder. For best appearance it is important that the girl's legs be arched out and that she keep her head up. This is a fairly tiring pose, and it is helpful to keep the boat speed up to lessen drag and for the boy to keep the arm that holds the towbar straight to lessen fatigue.

The transition from the forward layout to a "cross-arm carry" is quite rapid, but some care must be taken to avoid having it continue right into the water. The girl reaches over with one arm around the boy's neck, turns slightly, and swings into a cross-arm position. The boy must cushion the swing to avoid loss of balance. The resulting cross-arm carry is a very stable position and can be used as an excellent landing pose or for rhythmic skiing across the boat wakes.

The "human towbar" is an impressive trick that is not only a form of carry but also a novel method of tow.

The easiest way to accomplish this maneuver is to start with

The human tow:

331. Riding the same pair of skis . . .

332. . . . Paula turns around to face Rit . . .

333. . . . clasps her hands behind his neck . . .

334. . . . and jumps up to lock her legs around his waist.

335. Paula leans back, grabs the handle, and Rit eases the rope out.

336. When Rit lets go, Paula becomes the human tow.

both partners standing on one pair of skis. The girl then turns around to face her partner by reaching back to put one arm around his neck and on the count of three quickly switches her feet to the opposite skis. Then, with most of her weight being supported by her arms around the boy's neck, she jumps up to lock her legs around his waist. She leans back against her partner's arms and reaches to grasp the handle. Her partner braces her back and at the same time leans forward and *eases* the rope out. When the girl has absorbed the full towing load, her partner can straighten up. Considerable care should be taken to ease the rope out slowly, and the trick should not be done in rough water due to the danger of catching a wave in the towing position.

The recovery merely reverses the procedure, with the boy reaching forward to brace his partner's back and then regaining the tow-bar.

Landing from a doubles ride is much the same as coming in on a regular pair of skis except that care must be taken to avoid dropping the girl. One of the prettiest landings is obtained by approaching in a cross-arm carry and releasing the girl's legs just as the motion stops, to allow both to end standing side by side.

All mixed doubles maneuvers may be accomplished on one ski as well as on two, provided that the carrying partner is a steady one-ski performer. It is best to use a very wide ski, such as a jumping ski, and to put on a rear toe binder rather than to use a slalom ski. The boat speed should be about five miles per hour faster than with two skis, to lessen drag.

Have someone watch your routines to comment on which poses look good and which ones need improvement. Minor changes in hand position and poses can make a tremendous difference to your act.

SIDE-BY-SIDE TRICKS:

"Side-by-side" tricks depend on careful synchronization of the skiers' moves to make them effective. Fairly simple tricks can be put together into an interesting routine by coordinating the partners' moves: Skiers' salutes, crossing the wake, wake tricks, and toehold turns can be put together using your own counting technique to time the moves. Toehold turns on a single ski can be extremely graceful when used as a side-by-side maneuver.

The prime limitation to side-by-side tricks is the skiers' individual skiing abilities. Here the skiers' abilities are in sharp focus, and a great deal of skill is needed to put together an act involving tricks such as toehold turns, since each skier must be able to do them well before putting them together in a routine.

One precaution should be taken when skiing "side by side." Make sure that the ropes are no more than eight inches different in length. Otherwise, should a skier on a long rope fall, that rope might entangle the remaining skier.

SPECIALTY ACTS:

Specialty acts are many and varied, but they are usually attempted only by skiers with considerable individual abilities who have mastered the basic mixed doubles maneuvers. Such acts could include side-by-side barefooting, performing on shoe skis, and routines involving the jump as part of the over-all performance.

If both skiers are experienced ski jumpers, a great deal can be added to the act by using side-by-side jumps.

CONCLUSION:

This has been just a glimpse into the many possibilities of doubles skiing. Get out on the water and double your skiing fun.

337. Kite flying is tricky, but when you know what you're doing, it can be exciting fun. Flier of lower left kite is doing a front body swing. Girl in center is in standard kite flying position. Right kite flier is holding a left layout. (Courtesy Weyer's Aqua Products, Inc.)

CHAPTER THIRTEEN

Kite Flying

Kite flying was no doubt invented by some enterprising daredevil looking for kicks. Back in the early 1950s when it all started, it was dangerous, because the contraptions they called "kites" weren't half as safe as what Ben Franklin flew over two hundred years ago in a thunderstorm. Bolted, pasted, and wired haphazardly together, the first skier-carrying kites were constructed of wood frames covered by heavy canvas. In those days, malfunctioning or disintegrating kites caused bad crashes and, needless to say, serious injuries. But things have changed since then.

Today's kite frames are constructed of lightweight yet tremendously strong seamless aluminum alloy tubing covered with non-absorbent, tough, light nylon or Orlon. Reliable safety releases and flying harnesses are now standard, recommended equipment. Put all these together with common sense, a competent driver (he'd better be your best friend), and a powerful towboat in perfect condition—not to mention good weather conditions—and you *might* be able to fly a kite safely! This isn't intended to scare you, but when you are dealing with something that could possibly drop you from over a hundred feet in the air, you should at least treat it with respect.

THE PRINCIPLE OF KITE FLIGHT:

As is true of a toy kite, a man-carrying kite is lifted by air currents causing a difference in air pressure on opposite sides of the covering or "sail." The amount of lift generated is determined by the airspeed and sail area. Other relevant factors are the placement of the flier and the flying angle of the kite, known as "angle of attack," which is mainly determined by where the towline is attached to the kite.

THE KITE:

Kites generally come in two sizes: fourteen feet long by twelve feet wide, and sixteen feet long by fourteen feet wide. Use the proper size for your weight, taking the horsepower of the towboat into consideration as follows:

RECOMMENDED KITE SIZES

Flier's Weight	50-Hp Outboards	85–125 Hp Outboards	130 Hp and Over Inboards and Twin Outboards
80–150 lbs.	14'×12'	14'×12'	14'×12'
135–190 lbs.	16'×14'	14'×12'	14'×12'
175–225 lbs.	16'×14'	16'×14'	14'×12'
225 lbs. and over			16'×14'

Choose a well-tested kite constructed of seamless aluminum alloy tubing with reinforced joints having a minimum of two set screws, rivets, or other "locking" features to prevent them from coming apart under stress (see Diagram P).

Most kite sails are lashed to the frame by means of a single sail cable. However, on occasion rubbing and wear can lead to cable breakage. Depending on where this breakage occurs, and what part of the sail is loosened, a bad crash could result. Jim Weyer, a noted kite flier and mechanical engineer, has now designed a four-piece sail cable, drastically reducing wear because the separate cables needn't be forced through as many cable guides. Should one cable break, only one-fourth of the sail would partially collapse, and a controlled landing could still be made. Sail tension is usually adjusted by tightening or loosening the rope between the sail and the rear crossbar.

The flier literally hangs from a trapeze bar with which he controls the kite. The trapeze bar assembly must be safe and

P   KITE FRAME
(Sail and bridle omitted for clarity)

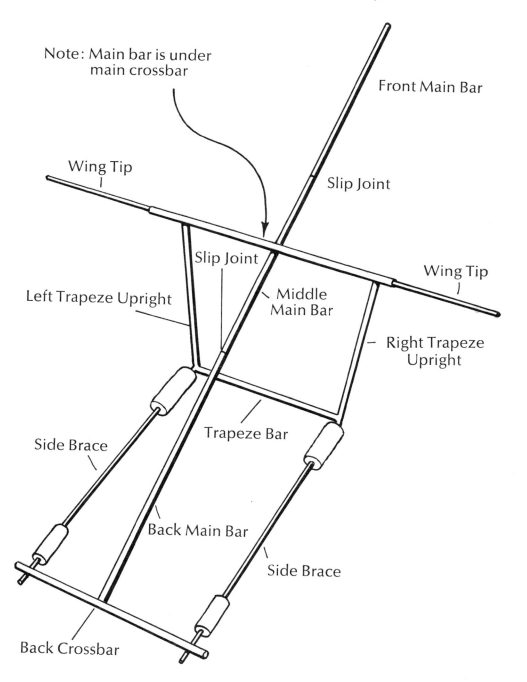

Note: Main bar is under
main crossbar

Front Main Bar

Wing Tip

Slip Joint

Slip Joint

Left Trapeze Upright

Middle
Main Bar

Wing Tip

Right Trapeze
Upright

Side Brace

Trapeze Bar

Back Main Bar

Side Brace

Back Crossbar

rigid. Gas- and oil-resistant styrofoam floats are mounted near each end of the side braces to enable the kite to float at a proper angle for easy deep-water starts.

The main towrope is attached to a four-point bridle fixed to the ends of the trapeze bar and main crossbar. This four-point bridle system (which is adjustable) 1. Keeps the kite from flying too high, limiting the rope angle to sixty degrees; 2. With adjustment allows for flying in gusty or adverse weather (but this isn't recommended); or 3. Can be used as an altitude control, by decreasing the angle of attack.

THE TOWROPE:

For your first flight, use a 100- to 125-pound towrope of 2000- to 2200-pound test diamond braid polyethylene line. Since this material stretches, it should not be used for lines over two hundred feet long, because its elasticity would produce a "Yo-Yo" effect. If longer lengths are desired (only when you become an expert), use a 2200-pound test steel aircraft cable. Never allow any knots to form in your towline, because weak spots develop at these points. Don't take chances with fraying ropes or ropes having broken strands.

THE QUICK BOAT RELEASE:

An absolute necessity is a quick release, which is placed immediately between the boat's rope hitch and the boat end of the tow rope. By pulling a small release line, the towrope is instantly freed from the boat. The observer in the boat must always hold the release line loosely but be alert to release the kite immediately in the event of emergency, or upon signal from the flier when he is taxiing back to the dock.

THE SAFETY HARNESS:

A safety harness is strongly recommended for all kite fliers. Attached to the center of the trapeze bar, the harness (not the flier's arms) supports his body weight, enabling him to use his arms entirely for kite control.

The quick release: This is a must for kite flying, and should be connected between the ski tow hitch of the boat and the towrope.

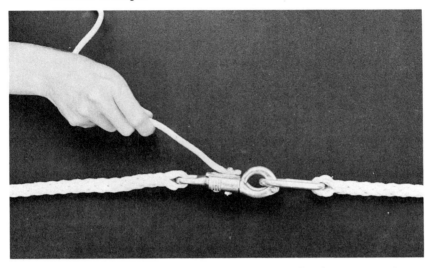

338. When the observer or "pin man" pulls the safety line . . .

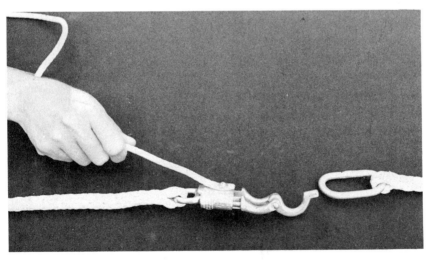

339. . . . the release opens, separating the towrope from the boat. (Courtesy Weyer's Aqua Products, Inc.)

Always see to it that your harness is *comfortable*. An uncomfortable harness can mean the difference between an enjoyable and a very unpleasant flight. A poor harness could actually cut off circulation in your legs, possibly jeopardizing your safety. A quick release mechanism is usually sewn into the harness strap between the flier and the trapeze bar. By simply pulling a release latch, you can immediately separate from the kite. The harness strap which connects to the trapeze bar should be properly adjusted so that your biceps are parallel to the trapeze bar during flight.

SKIS AND LIFE VEST:

Any conventional pair of water skis can be used for kite flying, but most experts prefer short, lightweight, standard skis to avoid wind resistance when airborne. Some even use short, wide trick skis because they are so light.

Always wear a sturdy life jacket or jumping vest. A ski belt is *not* sufficient for kite flying.

THE TOWBOAT:

A kite exerts approximately the same drag as three water skiers of the same weight as the flier. A fifty-horsepower outboard motor mounted on a short, wide-transomed boat provides the *minimum* power needed for proper kite towing, but more powerful, heavier boats are recommended. Fast, highly maneuverable inboards do the job best.

Jim Weyer made actual in-flight measurements of the pull on the towline using the same person skiing and kite flying:

	Skiing	*Kite Flying*
Normal tension (1 or 2 skis)	80–100 lbs.	200–300 lbs.
Slalom (1 ski)	0–300 lbs.	200–400 lbs.
Normal maximum tension (1 ski)	300 lbs.	400 lbs.

It is interesting to note that the normal kite-towing tension is *less* than the maximum pull exerted by a slalom skier.

A pickup boat should always be present in case of emergency or to assist the flier when he is in the water. It should trail the towboat but stay well out to the side of the kite.

BOAT DRIVER AND "RELEASE MAN" OR "PIN MAN":

Your driver should be an experienced kite flier or water ski boat driver, very familiar with the throttle and handling characteristics of the *particular towboat used.*

In towing a kite, the driver must frequently glance over his shoulder to keep an eye on the kite; for basically it is he who controls its altitude by increasing or decreasing the boat speed. When towing a novice flier, keep him low so you can land him immediately should a problem arise. A driver should always signal his intention to change course and should make turns gradually.

The observer, or "release man" or "pin man," should also be dependable, familiar with kite flying, and well versed in the flier's ability and signals. He pulls the safety release mechanism should the occasion arise, following these basic rules:

1. Release the kite on signal from the flier, when he is taxiing in for a landing.
2. If a crash is inevitable, pull the safety release when the flier touches the water, or just a split second before.
3. Never let the kite drag in the water still attached to the boat.
4. Never release the flier when he is airborne.

When taxiing the kite flier back to shore, the driver should slow down to ten to fifteen miles per hour. Driving too fast at the time of release could spill the skier.

Experts feel that even if a kite loses control (oscillating or diving), the driver *should not stop the boat,* but instead should throttle back gradually, making sure to keep some tension on the towrope.

KITE FLIER'S SIGNALS:

Everyone in your kite flying team should know the following signals by heart:

1. Nodding head: "Yes. Faster. More speed."
2. Shaking head from side to side: "No. Slow down."
3. Tilting head far back: "Reverse direction. Turn around."
4. Turning head to left: "Turn left."

5. Turning head to right: "Turn right."
6. Crossed skis: "Altitude okay."
7. Hard abrupt nod of head forward: "Release kite."

YOUR FIRST FLIGHT:

Pick a day when the wind speed is less than ten miles per hour and not gusty. Start from waist-deep water, or from a sitting position off a dock or platform. Either way is very easy. If starting from a dock, make sure there are no projections on it that could snag the sides or rear of the kite as it slides off the edge. Before you start, connect your safety harness to the trapeze bar.

Make your start as you normally would on standard water skis, holding onto the trapeze bar. When you are planing, steady the kite with your hands and signal the boat team to increase speed until the kite actually holds itself up with you skiing beneath it merely steadying it.

Practice taxiing around this way for a while, swinging back and forth inside the wake, maneuvering by banking the kite (dipping first one wing tip, then the other).

TAKING OFF:

Signal the boat to head into the wind, and when that is done, to increase speed. As soon as you become airborne, the driver should ease up on the throttle to prevent your going much higher than five to ten feet off the water. Keep the kite as level and as steady as possible *for the entire flight*.

CONTROLLING THE KITE:

The secret of kite control is to make very quick, small corrections. Keep your body directly under the center of the trapeze bar. Do not swing under it. Control the kite with your arms by pulling down on one side and pushing up on the other. Let the harness support your weight and simultaneously act as a pivot point.

THE LANDING:

Always keep you ski tips up to prevent them from digging in when touching the water. Kite landings are usually very soft,

but should you descend fast, absorb the shock naturally by "giving" in the knees. An experienced boat driver can land a flier like a feather. Your kite may be reused immediately, even if it is wet. If you follow all these instructions carefully, you'll have a thrilling and enjoyable flight.

OSCILLATION:

Inexperienced kite fliers often encounter oscillation caused by undercontrol (not correcting enough) or overcontrol (correcting too much). Either can result in the kite's rolling back and forth uncontrollably, with each tilting roll becoming more pronounced.

If a novice flier begins oscillating, the driver should immediately slow down the boat to land him quickly on the water. If the driver doesn't react instantly, the flier will most certainly end up swimming. For this reason novices should be flown no higher than ten feet until they can control the kite.

If the flier's problem is undercontrol, he may be shifting his body from side to side. This is wrong. He should control the kite with his *arms* and keep his body directly below the center of the trapeze bar.

Overcontrol is caused by correcting too much. Should the kite tilt to one side, immediately pull down on that side and push up on the other, but as soon as the kite reacts to your efforts, end the correction; otherwise you may have to correct in the opposite direction, and so on. Each time you overcorrect, the error (and the oscillation) will increase.

The best remedies for overcontrol are: 1. Begin your correction immediately; 2. Don't correct too much or too long, and 3. Try to stay calm and relaxed.

OTHER BASIC HINTS:

Just before takeoff your skis will ride very lightly on top of the water. At this stage, skis may have a tendency to catch in the water, thereby coming off your feet. This friction or suction can be broken by springing slightly into the ascent. When flying low, always keep your ski tips pointing up, out of harm's way. Should you lose a ski, don't worry; it is easier to land on one ski than you might think, because much of your body weight is supported by the kite's lift. This will rarely happen anyway.

ONE WORD OF CAUTION:

Generally speaking, don't fly the kite during poor weather conditions or when the water is crowded, with many boats in the area. Pursue this sport with other mature, sensible, experienced fliers and boat drivers. Always double-check your equipment before flying, and rehearse your flight path, directions, and signals with your driver and release man. Make sure the boat has enough gas!

340. A beautiful back layout. (Courtesy Cypress Gardens)

OFFICIAL TOURNAMENT LAYOUT OF KITE SLALOM COURSE

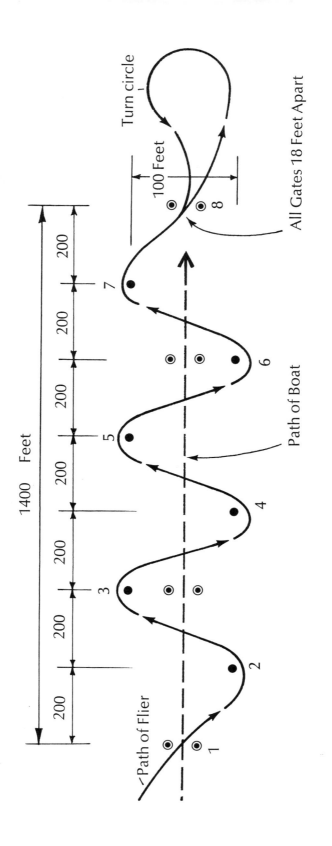

Turn circle

100 Feet

All Gates 18 Feet Apart

1400 Feet

200 200 200 200 200 200 200

Path of Flier

Path of Boat

⊙ ⊙ Boat Gates

● Slalom Buoy or Geyser

Q

Never use excessive rope lengths or fly over land, other boats, or swimmers. Remember that showing off often backfires.

KITE COMPETITION:

The American Water Ski Association sanctions kiting tournaments having slalom and trick kiting events. Trick kiting involves holding the body in various gymnastic positions when flying. In some of these positions, the kite may be controlled with one hand, with the toes, or with no part of the body touching the trapeze bar (the skier hanging by the harness strap). There are approximately forty tricks in this event, executed either on or hanging from the trapeze bar. Some examples are: turns, body swings, layouts, phalanges, tucks, rollovers, toe hangs, knee hangs, spiders, and bar swans.

Slalom kiting is very similar to slalom skiing, although the dimensions of the course are different (see Diagram Q).

To make a slalom turn in the air, you must bank the kite, thereby causing a sharp loss in altitude. An experienced slalom kiter can bank his kite almost ninety degrees and drop as much as seventy feet, simultaneously slipping in a sideward direction. As he recovers (hopefully before hitting the water), his momentum brings him into a fast ascent on the other side of the course (or wake). Experienced slalom kiters develop this rhythm and timing to be at their highest point as they round the gates and at their lowest point directly over the center of the wake.

In official tournaments, the AWSA used geysers of water as "slalom buoys," to enable both the flier and the judges to see the slalom course easily.

If you want more information about kite competition, write the American Water Ski Association for its booklet, *Official Kite Flying Rules.*

CHAPTER FOURTEEN

Para-Sailing

When France's Pierre Lemoigne invented the "parachute that goes up," little did he foresee that water skiers throughout the world would become customers. Flown like a kite behind a towing vehicle, the ascending parachute or Para-Sail lets air spill through slots in its canopy, creating a low-pressure area above it which produces an aerodynamic lift causing it to rise. Decreasing the towing speed or stopping altogether causes the Para-Sail to descend gently back to earth. The "Para-Sailor," with no strain on his body, hands, or feet, is merely a passenger enjoying the thrill of rising a hundred or more feet above the earth's surface and floating there until he drifts back to earth. He may even take a camera aloft to photograph the towboat or the view.

The Para-Sail is designed to carry between eighty and 225 pounds at air speeds from ten to twenty miles per hour. Since the Para-Sail must always take off into the wind, air speed should be calculated by adding the wind speed and the speed of the towing vehicle. (Naturally, if there is no wind, the Para-Sail can be taken aloft in any direction.)

Para-Sailing requires lots of room. Generally speaking, don't Para-Sail unless you can head into the wind for at least one-half mile with plenty of room to turn the boat at both ends. An adequately powered towboat and a safety or pickup boat are absolutely required. For launching, use the widest beach available (seventy-five feet or more) with at least fifty feet depth and absolutely no obstructions such as rocks, trees, bushes, or fence posts. The launching area should face directly into the wind.

THE PARA-SAIL:

Wetting the nylon Para-Sail canopy and its harness will not appreciably affect its flight characteristics. It may be reused while wet. After using a Para-Sail in salt water, however, promptly rinse it in fresh water to prevent corrosion of the hardware and to keep salt deposits from forming on the fabric. Dry it out thoroughly prior to folding and storage. Don't hang or dry the canopy in direct sunlight, as prolonged exposure to the sun may damage the nylon.

THE TOWBOAT:

The towboat should have seventy-five horsepower as a minimum, although much more horsepower is recommended. It should be capable of towing twelve hundred to fifteen hundred pounds easily at speeds up to thirty-five miles per hour. The towboat should have a very solid "beefed up" ski tow pylon or other acceptable towing bar, to withstand the towing strain. Should the towbar apparatus break or tear out during takeoff, injuries could result.

THE TOWROPE:

Use a dacron or polypropylene, thirty-five-hundred-pound-minimum, tensile-strength line (about seven-sixteenths inch in diameter), one hundred to three hundred feet long. In large, open areas longer towlines may be used, but remember that the weight of the extra towline must be borne by the Para-Sail. A safety release must be attached at the towbar (between the towbar and the boat end of the towline) which can be quickly released by the observer ("pin man") in the boat.

THE PARA-SAIL TEAM:

A team of six or more persons is needed for efficient Para-Sailing:
1. The driver of the towboat.
2. The observer in the towboat, also known as the "pin man."
3. The right-hand ground assistant for takeoff.
4. The left-hand ground assistant for takeoff.

5. The Para-Sailor.
6. The safety boat operator.

THE BOAT DRIVER AND "PIN MAN":

As in towing a kite, the driver of the boat towing a Para-Sail actually pilots and controls its whereabouts. He must not only be careful that his tow path is free of obstructions such as other boats, skiers, or docks, but must constantly observe the position of the Para-Sail. He should idle the boat directly into the wind until the towline is laid out its full length and then wait for a signal from one of the ground assistants to proceed with liftoff.

The observer or "pin man" also carries a great responsibility, at least as great as that of the driver. During takeoffs he must keep an eagle eye on the Para-Sailor, for should anything go wrong, he must instantly trip the safety release, freeing the towline from the boat, to prevent the Para-Sailor from being dragged across the ground or through the water. After a good flight, it is also his job to release the Para-Sailor at the proper place and point of time for his landing.

TAKING OFF AND LANDING THE PARA-SAILOR:

A smooth, constantly accelerating takeoff and climb without excessive speed is safest and most enjoyable for the Para-Sailor. Accelerate steadily until the Para-Sail reaches the desired height, then level off boat speed with gentle corrections on the throttle.

There are two ways to land the Para-Sailor. One is to slow the towboat gradually, allowing the Para-Sail to descend until the Para-Sailor's feet almost touch the water, at which point the rope from the boat is released by the "pin man," letting the Para-Sailor sink into the water.

The second way (and the one most often used by Para-Sailors over water) is to allow the Para-Sailor to climb to maximum or near maximum height (usually one hundred to 125 feet) and then release him from the boat, allowing the Para-Sail to float gently downward as an ordinary parachute would. In either case, the Para-Sailor gets a pleasant dunking, but in the "high release" method, care should be taken to preclude any possibility of the Para-Sailor drifting toward shore or near any boats, ramps, floating docks, etc.

DUTIES OF THE GROUND ASSISTANTS:

The ground assistants are responsible for laying out the canopy, fitting the harness, attaching the towline, and signaling the driver to "go." The harness and canopy should be laid out on the ground at the end of the launching area so that the towline and the towboat are facing into the wind. After making sure that the canopy is right side out, the assistants should straighten all lines and risers.

After checking the fit of the flight harness on the Para-Sailor, all hardware must be secured and the towrope attached to the connecting ring on the risers. The guide lines are held high by the ground assistants while waiting for the canopy to inflate.

When the ground assistants have checked that all lines are clear, that the air and water areas are free of traffic, and that the Para-Sailor is ready, they should first signal the boat driver to slowly take up the slack in the towline. When it becomes taut, they should signal the driver to accelerate. At this point both ground assistants and Para-Sailor should move forward with the canopy until it fully inflates. They must hold their guide lines evenly, making sure to release them simultaneously, and must step clear of the fully inflated canopy to assure a straight takeoff. If these are not done, a diagonal liftoff will result. A diagonal liftoff may also result if they allow the canopy to tilt to either side during the takeoff.

THE PARA-SAILOR:

The Para-Sailor should always wear a snug-fitting life vest or jump jacket under his flight harness. This harness, with all its buckles and other hardware, adds quite a bit of weight to the flier. Without the life vest, he'd find it hard to stay afloat after landing.

Once the Para-Sailor has gotten into the harness, he should check to see that all lines are straight and clear, and that the canopy is in correct position. All harness straps and buckles must be secure. On takeoff, the Para-Sailor may hold onto the towline attachment yoke forward of the snaps, but he should not disturb the lift risers going up to the canopy. If the takeoff is made into a gentle breeze, the canopy may fill and blossom even before the boat begins to accelerate. In such a case, the Para-Sailor may lift off immediately upon acceleration. If there is no breeze, the Para-Sailor should take two or three long strides after the towline is taut and the towboat has begun acceleration. The Para-Sailor should not try to aid liftoff by jumping or pulling up his feet. The canopy will do that.

IN FLIGHT:

During a perfectly still (windless) day, the Para-Sail can be kept aloft and towed in any direction almost indefinitely at a steady towing speed. If you wish to Para-Sail in a ten-mile-per-hour steady wind, for example, you may even tow it crosswind and with the wind, providing you increase the overwater towing speed so that the Para-Sail's *airspeed* remains constant.

Therefore, assuming that a lightweight Para-Sailor requires only fifteen-mile-per-hour *airspeed* to ascend, the towboat speed required to keep him aloft in a ten-mile-per-hour headwind would be only five miles per hour over the water. However, when the boat makes a turn going crosswind, it must begin to accelerate; and finally, when towing with the wind (toward the south), it must make up for the ten-mile-per-hour wind (blowing in that direction) plus the fifteen-mile-per-hour airspeed required by the Para-Sail to remain aloft—or it must attain a twenty-five-mile-per-hour towing speed.

The Para-Sailor can sideslip or steer his Para-Sail to a certain extent by pulling down on the risers on the side toward which he wishes to go. For instance, to turn right, he would grasp the risers on the right side and pull down on them until the Para-Sail responds. This action spills air from the right side of the canopy, causing it to move in that direction, but also losing some altitude in that direction.

Nevertheless, under no circumstances should the driver depend on the "steering ability" of the Para-Sailor.

THE PICKUP BOAT:

After the Para-Sail becomes airborne, the pickup boat should trail it at a safe distance, preferably two hundred feet to either side. The passengers of this boat should see to it that no other vessels cruise near or under the Para-Sail's path and should generally keep a sharp eye on the situation. After the Para-Sailor has landed in the water, the pickup boat should idle over to pick him up and help to retrieve the Para-Sail.

SAFETY HINTS:

Although Para-Sailing is basically safer than kite flying, any equipment, no matter how safe, can be used in a reckless and dangerous manner. Fly the Para-Sail only when conditions are safe and with a crew that understands its operation. Never Para-Sail on a busy Saturday or Sunday afternoon when the water is crowded with many boats and when curiosity seekers may unknowingly get in your way to see the "parachute that goes up." Don't fly the Para-Sail in turbulent or gusty winds or in any winds above fifteen miles per hour. Remember, in all cases, that the "pin man" does the final releasing when landing the Para-Sailor.

If the Para-Sail rotates more than forty-five degrees to either side, it should be released before the canopy has a chance to spill its air, causing a quick loss of altitude. As described in the second landing method, the Para-Sailor will then merely descend to the surface as if he had on a regular parachute.

For easy "floating" landings, a minimum altitude of forty to fifty feet should be attained before the towline is released.

In conclusion, lots of room, several reliable assistants, superior equipment, good weather conditions, and just plain common sense are the formula for safe Para-Sailing. Each of your Para-Sailing team should read and understand these instructions. Have fun.

CHAPTER FIFTEEN

Speed Skiing

Actually racing on skis, speed skiing can be separated into four groups.

1. Drag skiing, where skiers are timed and measured over a quarter-mile course. This takes a real daredevil, one in perfect shape. It is definitely not recommended for beginners. Racers have attained skiing speeds of up to 130 miles per hour.
2. Open course racing from point to point—usually done on large bodies of water or the ocean.
3. Closed course racing around a specific course marked out on the water. Contestants are divided into age classes for both men and women.
4. Marathon racing over very long distances: fifty miles up to hundreds of miles.

Speed skiing is most popular in California where the majority of the racing is done behind special SK Class or Super-Stock boats. These can cost up to $10,000 or more and can clock up to 150 miles per hour. It is very much a team sport. You can imagine how important a good driver and observer are, because at such high speeds one wrong move on their part can send the racer into a bad spill. The driver and observer must rigidly follow the racing rules laid down by the Pacific Coast Speedboat and Water Ski Association to maintain a course that does not block other boats.

Most racers use a racing ski that looks roughly like a very

long and heavy jumping ski. It has two binders and a deep tail
fin like a slalom ski and is ridden like a slalom ski, but with the
racer leaning quite a bit of his weight on his rear foot. Most
racing skis are seventy-five to eighty-five inches long. High-quality
binders are important because they should give some foot and
ankle support.

Naturally, a rugged, snug-fitting safety jacket must be worn
for racing. Some racers wear tight-fitting bathing caps or hoods
made of neoprene to protect their heads and ears should they fall.

All in all, speed skiing is a brace-yourself-and-hang-on-for-dear-
life sport which is rapidly growing out west. It is as safe as you
and your driver-observer team make it. Many skiers have fallen
at very high speeds and been unhurt, but none of them particularly liked the feeling.

CHAPTER SIXTEEN

How to Preserve the Life of Your Water Skis

Taking proper care of your water skis begins with proper preuse maintenance and "tender, loving care." Let's face it, water skis can take the punishment they are designed for, but why run them over rocks and sand? Or walk down the dock with them? They're built for skiing on water, and that's the only substance with which they should come into contact—except for jumping skis, which are designed to slide up ramp surfaces.

Most water skis are made of wood. Sometimes the wood is covered with melamine for greater durability. Recently fiberglass skis have made their debut. After buying a new pair of water skis and before your first time out, give them a good coat of Simoniz or similar wax. Waxing not only preserves the skis, but makes their bottoms smoother so that they will glide more effortlessly, with less resistance, over the water. Secondly, take a screwdriver and tighten all screws firmly by hand. (Those screws fastening rubber binder parts should not be overtightened.)

After using your water skis, don't just toss them down on sharp rocks or pebble beaches. Avoid getting sand into the adjustable binder parts. When you're not skiing, keep your water skis out of the sun and rain. Lay them in the shade or in a cool, dry place.

After a hard day's use, inspect your skis carefully to see if the finish has been scratched or chipped, creating dangerous slivers. If so, sand the rough spot slightly, or cut the sliver away with a razor blade. All scratches or bared wood should be systematically touched up with urethane, varnish, or paint. Then the skis should be waxed again. If this is not done promptly, the bare spots will absorb water, causing ugly dark marks, and damaging the wood. A small scratch or chip can lead to subsequent deterioration, delamination, or breaking.

Although fiberglass skis resist scratching and gouging better than wood, it's still a good idea to keep all surfaces smooth and free of scratches. Sanding with fine sandpaper and waxing usually does the trick. Should a fiberglass ski become clipped or gouged badly, it should be filled in with a good two-part epoxy resin, then sanded and repainted with special fiberglass paint.

BINDER MAINTENANCE:

Any sharp or protruding corner or edge should be filed or ground to a round bevel. Smooth out marred screw heads with emery cloth. If a side bar or rail shows any possibility of cutting your foot, paste a piece of rubber over it with contact cement. In case your foot does come in contact with that part, the rubber will cushion the blow. Sometimes even a piece of tape over the sharp edge helps. Should any screws pull out of the ski, fill the holes with glue and hardwood pegs, then redrill.

Check your toe and heel binders often for tears or other deterioration, and change them when necessary. Check all skegs or runners, whether slalom fins or wood fins, for proper attachment to the ski, and tighten their screws periodically.

Generally speaking, a defect in a water ski will show up during the first few hours' use. Bill Rutland, general manager of Cypress Gardens Skis, Inc., in an article about jumping skis, says: "Our experience has shown that in most instances, if a jumper is going to delaminate or pop out, it will do so within the first few times it is used off the ramp. Our slow-motion pictures have shown that the flexing of the tips of jumpers on impact with the water is almost unbelievable." He goes on to say, "Entire tips of jumpers have been known to disintegrate on impact. Skiers have been known to go right through the bottom of jumpers. This possibility, by the way, is the main reason why plate binders are used on jumpers. The plate is a safety factor in the event a jump ski fractures under the foot. A cracked jumper holds the same dangers as a cracked conventional ski, multiplied many times over." Personally, I find custom plate binders heavy and cumbersome and would much rather have my binders attached directly to the ski.

STORAGE OF WATER SKIS:

Store your water skis in a cool, dry place. Skis stored in damp cellars have a tendency to warp out of shape by the time spring rolls around again. On the other hand, don't store your skis too close to a furnace or in an abnormally hot room of your home. This might dry out the wood, causing the skis to become brittle, which increases their chances of breaking. If you have a favorite pair of trick skis or jumpers with just the right "arc" or "dihedral" or "rocker" and you want to make sure they'll be the same next year, put them in a press or clamp them together to preserve their exact shape.

REFINISHING SKIS:

When your skis need a "face-lifting," a few hours' work can put them right back in shape. First remove the binders and hardware. Fill all unnecessary or enlarged screw holes with glue and hardwood pegs. Plastic wood or an equivalent filler can also be used. Sand the entire ski with a medium-coarse sandpaper. Apply a good coat of sealer. Then resand, this time with fine sandpaper. Apply a good grade of varnish, urethane, or hard marine enamel, following the manufacturer's directions.

Then remount all hardware and binders, making sure to replace any torn or "doubtful" toe or heel pieces. While the binders are off, here's a good opportunity for you to eliminate foot slippage by sticking non-skid tape directly under where your feet stand on the skis. You'll be surprised at how much more control you'll have.

Treat your water skis with respect—as if they were one of your prized possessions; after all, look at the fun they give you.

IN CONCLUSION:

I hope you've gotten something out of this book, and that I've succeeded in "hooking you" on the sport of water skiing.

To get even more pleasure from water skiing, join your local ski club, your state federation, and the American Water Ski Association. AWSA publishes seven times yearly a fine magazine— *The Water Skier*—which will keep you abreast of worldwide skiing news. Annual membership is only ten dollars and includes a free subscription to *The Water Skier* magazine. AWSA also sells many hard-to-get items, such as official towropes, ramp wax, jump distance meters, and tournament kits, and distributes many free booklets on the various phases of water skiing.

Write to the American Water Ski Association, 7th Street and Avenue G, Southwest, Winter Haven, Florida 33880.

Born in Troy, New York, Al Tyll developed an early interest in sports through his father, who was a New England gymnastic champion. He water skied for the first time in 1954, but recalls of that experience, "I didn't even make it on the first try." His improvement was rapid, however, and soon he was attempting gymnastic tricks on water skis. He entered his first tournament in 1959, winning a number of second- and third-place honors that year and the next. In 1961 he began winning tournaments regularly (he didn't lose a single one in 1965), and he swept the National Men's Trick Skiing Championships in 1962, 1963, 1964, and 1965. After a two-year layoff, he returned to competition in 1968, winning the Eastern Regional Over-All Championship and the National Men's Tricks Championship. During the past few years he has held several trick clinics, and two of his students, Wayne Grimditch and Janie Peckinpaugh, have won national championships. Mr. Tyll and his wife, Chris (1968 Women's Eastern Regional Jumping Champion) and their daughter live at and ski on Bantam Lake in Connecticut.